An ICELAND Guide

Cooking from your Freezer

Mary Berry

A Martin Book

Published by Martin Books
an imprint of Woodhead-Faulkner Limited
Fitzwilliam House, 32 Trumpington Street
Cambridge CB2 1QY
for Iceland Frozen Foods Limited
Second Avenue, Deeside Industrial Park, Deeside, Clwyd

First published 1985

British Library Cataloguing in Publication Data
Berry, Mary, *1935-*
The Iceland guide to cooking from your freezer
1. Cookery (Frozen foods)
I. Title
641.5′55 TX828

ISBN 0 85941 317 9 (cased)
ISBN 0 85941 305 5 (paper)

Design and layout: Michael Leaman
Photography: Edmund Goldspink
Cover photograph of Mary Berry: Family Circle
Home economist: Elizabeth Holmes
Consultant home economist, Iceland Frozen Foods Limited: Wendy Strang
Stylist: Shân Lang
Illustrations: Helen Graham-Cameron
Typeset by Hands Fotoset, Leicester
Printed and bound in Great Britain by Springbourne Press Limited, Basildon, Essex

Contents

Preface

I can hardly remember my life without a freezer. It has certainly made me relax about entertaining and it is a joy to have something in the freezer for when the family is extended or friends drop in at short notice. When the children arrive back starving from a cricket match with two or three friends, it gives me peace of mind to know that there is nourishing soup, perhaps a lasagne or a quiche and lots of ice cream ready in the freezer.

I use my freezer as an extension to my store cupboard and fridge. I try hard to rotate the food in the freezer and not just to use the freezer as a bank as I used to do, hoarding the food rather like a squirrel and keeping it there far too long. There is no danger in doing this, of course, providing that the food is kept below freezing temperature (−18°C/0°F). It just doesn't taste quite so good after a couple of years, and loses some colour and texture.

I would like to thank Clare Blunt for assistance with research and recipe testing. We are great freezer fans as we both have hungry children to feed – all the family have enjoyed tasting the recipes!

Using the Freezer

BULK BUYING

I find it saves a great deal of time and petrol to buy food in bulk from the freezer centre. Buy what your family enjoys and is going to eat – the free-flow larger packs are cheaper and take up less space, but when trying a new product, it is best to buy a small pack first.

MICROWAVE COOKERS AND THE FREEZER

Microwave ovens are transforming the way we cook and make a perfect companion to the freezer. No more panic when you have forgotten to take something out of the freezer, or when unexpected guests arrive and you want to offer them a meal! Reheating and thawing in the microwave takes a fraction of the time normally needed.

The best plan is to take the food from the freezer and, if it is not already in dishes suitable for the microwave, to transfer it. (If you intend to use a microwave for thawing and reheating, it is practical to pack your cooked dishes in meal-sized microwave freezer containers, as bulk packs take longer to thaw and reheat.) If layered, separate the food as soon as possible. Cover and then defrost according to the chart in your microwave handbook. Defrosting times will vary according to the shape and size of the food, and it is a good idea to turn the food over or to stir it during this process. It is often necessary to leave the food to stand after thawing, before cooking and reheating. See your microwave handbook for instructions.

Vegetables can be cooked directly from frozen without thawing, but large pieces of meat and poultry must be completely thawed before beginning to cook, and the recommended standing times allowed. Small portions of soup, sauces and casseroles can be defrosted and heated simultaneously in the microwave.

Using the microwave with this book

The microwave instructions in this book are based on a 650-watt cooker and give approximate times for defrosting, standing and reheating dishes. All dishes are thawed on Defrost or Low (Power Level 3) and reheated on High (Power Level 8) or 90%, unless otherwise stated. Timings may vary according to the weight, shape and starting temperature of the food. If using a microwave oven of a higher or lower wattage than 650, timings will need to be altered accordingly.

Generally, it is much better to undercook dishes than overcook them, as they can easily be placed back in the microwave if extra cooking is needed. For each dish, transfer to a container suitable for the microwave if necessary and stir occasionally. (For larger items, such as chicken portions, move the food around so that the bones are near to the centre of the microwave.)

HOW TO PACK FOR THE FREEZER

Packing materials

There are many to choose from, but the important thing is to exclude as much air as possible from the package by wrapping it in freezer film, foil or thick polythene so that the food doesn't dry out. Polythene bags and polythene or foil containers are ideal. Choose the packaging most appropriate to the food. Some bags and boxes are coloured, which helps when identifying food in the freezer. (For example, I use red for meat, game and poultry, yellow for fruit, green for vegetables and blue for fish.)

Since space is often limited in a freezer, careful packaging is important. It helps to store all foods of the same type in the same basket, box or large coloured plastic bag in the freezer. I keep the foods that I use least often, such as turkey or game, at the back of an upright freezer or at the bottom of a chest freezer.

Polythene bags

These are good for all foods except liquids. For these, i.e. stocks, soups or casseroles, fit a bag in a polythene container or foil dish and pour in the liquid. Freeze until solid, then take out the 'square' bag and the dish is free again for use.

Use heavy gauge polythene bags for freezing to obtain the best results. To seal polythene bags, either use twist seals or tie a knot in the bag – this can be annoying to undo, however.

Polythene boxes

These are rigid boxes best used for liquids, soups, sauces, casseroles, ice cream and cakes. You can of course re-use plastic ice cream boxes.

Cling film

The heavy duty kind is best, and is especially made for the freezer. Wrap up larger items, joints of meat, chops and individual portions of food in cling film and then slip into a polythene bag for further protection.

Boil-in-bags

These are strong see-through bags for casseroles or food in sauces. The food is frozen in the bag and then reheated, still in the bag, in a pan of simmering water.

Foil

Use this to wrap items of food such as joints of meat, then pack again in a polythene bag.

Foil dishes

These are good for pies, cheesecakes, pâtés, etc., and for shaped food packs which have been moulded from polythene boxes and ovenproof dishes. They are also an ideal way to pack casseroles, stewed fruit and sauces.

To pack a casserole, cook and turn into a foil dish, and freeze until frozen solid. If you want to re-use the foil dish, first place a polythene bag in the dish and pour the cooked and cooled casserole into this. When frozen solid, remove the 'square' bag and the dish is free again for use. Use polythene boxes in the same way.

Sealing and labelling

Sealing is important to exclude the air. You can use pumps to remove the air, or, it is sometimes suggested, you can immerse the bag and its contents in a bowl of cold water and then tie a tie twist round the top. However, I find all this quite unnecessary – I simply fill the bag, smooth it with my hands to exclude as much air as possible and then seal it.

When using polythene boxes, I take care to choose ones with well-fitting lids and fill to not more than 1 inch (2.5 cm) from the top.

When labelling polythene bags I find it best to lie the bag flat before filling, in order to write on the details with a waterproof marker pen, i.e. '1 lb (450 g) young carrots, July 1984'. I also use a marker pen on polythene box lids and foil lids. (A little cleanser cream gets it off when cleaning them afterwards.) I use marker pens as I find that labels so often fall off.

HOW TO FREEZE FOOD

All foods can be frozen but some freeze better than others. If your freezer has fast freeze control, use it when freezing over 3 lb (1.3 kg) of food at one go. This control overrides the thermostat, keeping the freezer extra cold. Put on for 1 hour before freezing and turn off once the food is frozen solid. If you are freezing hot food, it is economical to allow it to cool first, thus saving on fuel bills.

I now try to turn the food in my freezer around far more quickly than I used to. In this way the food is fresher and I am using my freezer to full advantage. Small amounts of food freeze less well than large amounts.

Freezing prepared food

To freeze prepared food, such as soups, casseroles and cooked dishes, cool the food in the larder or kitchen and then place in the fridge until stone-cold. Wrap or cover and then freeze. You can also freeze the food in the dish it is going to be served in (see *Foil dishes,* page 7, and the instructions to the recipes later in this book).

Freezing sauces

Most sauces freeze well, but it helps to beat them after thawing and during reheating to avoid separation.

Freezing meat and poultry

Wrap up and pack in strong polythene, excluding all the air. If there is a bone, wrap its end in foil to avoid puncturing the wrapping. Pack in convenient family-sized portions, with some individual packages of chops and chicken. Stuffed joints should be kept frozen for half the time of unstuffed.

Freezing bread, cakes, puddings and pastries

Complete the item, then wrap according to type (detailed instructions follow the recipes later in this book). If the food is decorated or delicate, first open-freeze on a plate or rack until frozen solid and then wrap in cling film and a polythene bag.

Freezing dairy produce

1 Cream

Only freeze rich cream such as double and whip this first or the result may be a little granular. Less rich cream curdles on thawing. Clotted cream freezes well. To freeze whipped cream, either use to sandwich cakes together or pipe as rosettes on to silicone paper. Freeze these until solid and then pack in polythene boxes, interleaving the layers with foil or cling film.

2 Milk

Freeze only cartons of homogenised milk and use within 6 weeks. Ordinary milk separates on thawing.

3 Eggs

Don't freeze eggs in the shell as they crack on thawing. There are two ways in which eggs can be frozen:

(i) Whole, lightly beaten.
(ii) Separated, with the yolks blended and ½ teaspoon salt or sugar added per 2 yolks. (Use salt for savoury recipes and sugar for sweet, and label accordingly.)

4 Cheese

Cheeses with low fat, e.g. cottage cheese and some cream cheese, are watery when thawed. Cheddar cheese is inclined to be crumbly when thawed, but this is good for cooking. Grated cheese can be frozen successfully. Rich cheeses such as Brie and Camembert freeze well if frozen when ripe.

5 Butter

Keep salted butter up to 6 months, unsalted butter up to 1 year. Keep both well wrapped in foil or a polythene bag.

6 Margarine and white fats

There is no need to freeze these as they keep well in the fridge. They can be frozen if desired, however, as for butter.

7 Yogurt

Most commercial varieties will freeze well, but natural unsweetened yogurt will separate and a teaspoon of sugar should be added. There are some ready-frozen commercial varieties with added stabilisers. Home-made yogurt separates on thawing and freezing is not recommended.

Freezing fish

Only freshly caught fish should be frozen, whether from the sea or river. Clean and gut straight away and wrap either whole or in cutlets or steaks, according to the size of the fish. Large, whole fish keep best. Wrap well in foil and then put in a polythene bag.

Freezing vegetables

Freeze these when young and tender. Vegetables are always best if blanched before freezing. Blanching times vary from 1-10 minutes, according to type (see chart below). Blanch the vegetables in boiling water, then drain and quickly cool.

For free-flow frozen vegetables (for instance, free-flow sprouts) spread out on a tray, open-freeze until each item has frozen solid, then pack in large polythene bags and return to the freezer. Then, when the vegetables are wanted, take out exactly the number you need for that meal and then seal the bag and return it to the freezer. Or you can freeze in polythene containers.

Vegetable	*Recommended blanching time*
artichokes, globe	6–8 minutes
aubergines	4 minutes
beans:	
french, whole	1–2 minutes
runner, sliced	1–2 minutes
broad, shelled	1–2 minutes
beetroot:	
small, whole	5–10 minutes
large	cook until tender, slice and freeze
broccoli:	
thin-stemmed	1 minute
medium-stemmed	2 minutes
brussels sprouts	1½–3 minutes
carrots, sliced	3–4 minutes
cauliflower, cut in sprigs	2 minutes
celery, sliced	2 minutes
corn on the cob, medium-size	5 minutes
courgettes, sliced	1 minute
onions:	
small, whole	4 minutes
sliced	2 minutes
parsnips, cubed	2 minutes
peas	1 minute
peppers, sliced	3 minutes
spinach leaves	2 minutes
turnips, diced	2 minutes

Freezing fruit

Choose fruit in prime ripe condition without blemishes. (Any damaged fruit can be stewed and then frozen.) Freeze straight after picking. Freeze according to type: some fruits, such as raspberries, loganberries, blackberries, gooseberries, currants and small strawberries can be frozen just as they are in polythene bags or boxes once they have been prepared, i.e. hulled, topped and tailed. Others, such as apples, plums and pears, need added sugar or sugar syrup. Fruit purées freeze well, e.g. apple, raspberry, strawberry, gooseberry, rhubarb and apricot purées.

FOODS THAT DO NOT FREEZE WELL

Salad ingredients

Crisp salads – lettuce, watercress, celery, cucumber, tomatoes and radishes – are limp and mushy when thawed, and could only be used in soup making. In the case of tomatoes, thaw for 10 minutes, then slip the skins off and use in casseroles.

Potatoes

Some types are tough when thawed, even after blanching. It is best to cook them and make croquettes or to freeze mashed potatoes and use for pie toppings. Potato chips freeze well, however – fry until tender but not brown, cool quickly and then pack.

Whole, hard-boiled eggs

These are leathery when thawed, though hard-boiled eggs can be included in a frozen egg mousse or fish pie, if chopped first.

Mayonnaise

This curdles on thawing.

Custard

This separates out and has a curdled effect when thawed. Canned custard freezes well and can be used on frozen trifles. Egg custard cannot be frozen.

Creams, milk and cheese

See the dairy produce section on pages 9–10.

Gelatine

Plain jellies do not freeze, and collapse on thawing. Mousses that include other ingredients, e.g. whipped cream, freeze well for short periods.

HOW TO THAW FOOD

For most foods it is best to thaw them slowly in a cool kitchen or larder. In the case of raw meat I try to think a couple of days ahead and thaw in the refrigerator, as this way you get less drip from the meat. If you have one, a microwave is invaluable for thawing food.

Cooking straight from the freezer

This is ideal for small items that are to be served hot, e.g. small sausage rolls, some pastry items, beefburgers, oven chips, croquettes, frozen vegetables and croissants. For large items such as a large deep meat pie or joint, the oven uses more fuel and often one ends up with an over-cooked outside and cool centre to the dish. However, in an emergency, anything except for poultry can be cooked from frozen – in most cases just lower the oven temperature and cook for longer.

Soups, sauces and prepared dishes

Ideally, thaw these in the refrigerator or at room temperature overnight. If time is short, gently reheat from frozen in a non-stick pan, stirring all the time.

Raw meat and poultry

Thaw either in the refrigerator or in the kitchen, covered.

Although meat – but not poultry – can be cooked from frozen, I find it not so tender.

Large birds are best thawed at room temperature: allow 3 hours per lb (450 g). Don't forget to take out the giblets once thawed for stock. Also, remember to keep thawing meat well away from pets!

Bread

This thaws quickly at room temperature. Rolls take 30 minutes, loaves 2 hours. If liked, frozen sliced bread can be toasted for speed. It can also be fried from frozen.

Cakes and biscuits

Thaw at room temperature. Unwrap to make sure that the wrapping doesn't stick but keep loosely covered with cling film to keep in the moisture. If time is short, biscuits can be thawed in the oven and then cooled on a wire rack until crisp.

Dairy produce

Thaw in the refrigerator.

Ice cream

Only experience tells you how long to thaw home-made ice cream and sorbets, as it depends on the fat content. Rich creamy ones, such as the recipe on page 66, can be served after thawing for 5–10 minutes.

Fish

Leave fish to thaw overnight in the refrigerator or, if time is short, at room temperature. The time will vary according to the thickness of the fish.

A dinner party from the freezer: Prawn Cocktail (page 25), Beef Olives (page 34), Pineapple Mousse (page 65) and Shortbread Fingers (page 88).

Vegetables

These are best not thawed – just plunge into a small quantity of boiling salted water and boil until cooked but still crisp and with a good texture. The only exception is corn-on-the-cob, as this is thick and so may need boiling for slightly longer, immersed in boiling water.

Fruit

Thaw fruit slowly at room temperature or in the refrigerator if time allows. Free-flow frozen soft fruit takes only 20 minutes or so to thaw if spread out, whereas a deep pack of frozen solid fruit can take all day, even in the kitchen.

REFREEZING

As a general rule, providing that it is perfectly fresh and has been thawed correctly, most food can safely be refrozen.

Refreezing meat and fish

Once meat or fish has been defrosted it should be cooked before refreezing. For example, use thawed frozen mince to make Shepherd's pie. Or, with fish such as frozen cod, thaw the fish, poach it, add it to a white sauce with other ingredients and top with mashed potato or pastry.

Refreezing cakes and pastry

If these are fresh and well wrapped, the results are satisfactory.

Refreezing ice cream and cream

Never refreeze thawed ice cream. If partially melted, remove the liquid before refreezing. Avoid refreezing cream as it will separate.

Refreezing fruit and vegetables

This is not a good idea as they lose texture and colour if just simply thawed, refrozen and then cooked. However, if once thawed they are cooked and used in a pie or sauce, they can be refrozen successfully.

DEFROSTING THE FREEZER

Ideally, choose a time when the freezer is not too full, as then you have less to lift out. I usually do mine before the summer glut of fruit and before the school holidays when the children come home.

1 Unplug the freezer.
2 Cover the floor with folded newspaper, an area the size of your freezer. Take out the baskets and boxes of frozen food, making sure that any ice cream is in the centre of the pile (or transfer it to the freezer section of the fridge). Cover the pile with old blankets or sleeping bags.
3 Put a large bowl or bucket of extremely hot water in the freezer. Put several sheets of newspaper in the bottom of the freezer and stand the bowl on it, then close the freezer lid or door. Leave for about 1 hour. If the freezer is very icy, change the water or reheat it.
4 Sort out the food into logical baskets or boxes ready to restock the freezer.
5 Remove the water container when the ice has melted. Start the mopping up with cloths or a sponge. (The newspaper will have sopped up some of the melting ice from the freezer, too.) You may have to remove the last bit of ice with a plastic spatula. Wipe the freezer dry and clean the outside.
6 Switch on the freezer.
7 Restock the freezer after 30 minutes.

STORAGE CHART

Food	**Recommended storage time**
vegetable and fruit	
most vegetables	12 months
raw mushrooms	1 month
cooked mushrooms	3 months
onions	3–6 months
herbs	6 months
most fruit	12 months
unstoned fruit	3 months
fruit purées	12 months
fruit pies	6 months
meat, poultry and fish	
uncooked meats:	
lamb, joints	8 months
lamb, small portions	3 months
pork, joints	6 months
pork, small portions	3 months
beef	8 months
veal	6 months
mince	3 months
offal	3 months
bacon, vacuum-packed	5 months
sausages	2 months
uncooked poultry:	
chicken	12 months

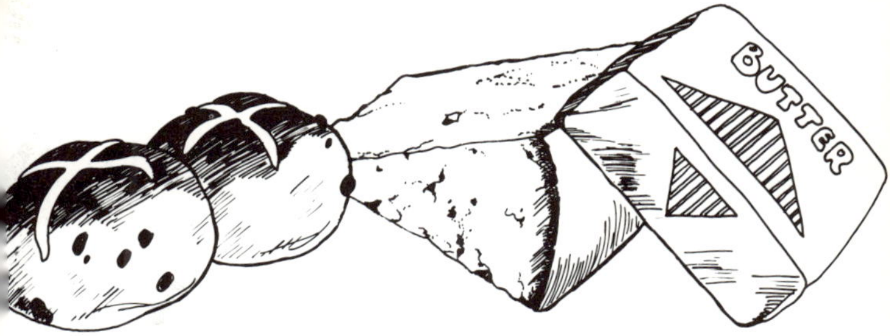

duck	6 months
game	12 months
uncooked fish:	
white fish	3 months
whole salmon	6 months
oily fish	2 months
shellfish	1 month
prepared food	
cooked dishes, e.g. pies and casseroles	3 months
sauces	1–3 months
pâtés	1 month
cakes, bread and pastry	6 months
puddings	1–3 months
pizza, unbaked	3 months
sandwiches and scones	2 months
croûtons and breadcrumbs	6 months
dairy produce	
cream	3 months
commercially bought frozen yogurt	1 month
unsalted butter	12 months
salted butter	6 months
margarine	6 months
homogenised milk	6 weeks
hard cheese	3 months
cream cheese	6 weeks
Camembert and Brie	3 months
ice cream	2 months
eggs	2 months

Good Beginnings

It is often convenient to divide soups up into small portions of, say, ½–¾ pint (300–450 ml). Make sure that you leave enough room in the containers for expansion and add any milk or cream when you are reheating. Sometimes you will find that it is necessary to add a little extra stock after freezing, as the soups do thicken up. A recipe for stock has also been included since many recipes use stock and it is lovely to have a home-made one ready in the freezer.

Pâtés can be frozen in the containers in which they were cooked, but if you think the containers will be needed, turn the frozen pâtés out and wrap in a double thickness of foil and a polythene bag. Pâtés are best thawed overnight in the refrigerator, and then I like to leave them at room temperature for about an hour before serving, as this allows the flavours to breathe.

CHICKEN STOCK

This is a very useful product to keep in the freezer, as it is frequently used in recipes. Chicken carcasses may be stored in the freezer until you have enough to make a large pot of stock. Beef stock may be made in the same way using bones from a roast joint or fresh bones from the butcher, but it is best to brown the bones first in the oven to give colour and add flavour.

2–3 frozen chicken carcasses
2 carrots, scraped and sliced
2 onions, sliced
1 bay leaf
1 teaspoon mixed dried herbs
¼ teaspoon ground mace
1 teaspoon salt
¼ teaspoon pepper

Break up the hard frozen chicken roughly with a rolling

pin, put in a large saucepan with all the remaining ingredients and add sufficient cold water to cover. Bring to the boil, cover the saucepan with a lid and simmer for about 1 hour. Strain the stock, discarding the bones and vegetables and leave to cool.

To freeze: *measure the stock into conveniently sized containers, cover, label and freeze. When solid the stock may be transferred to polythene bags, sealed and labelled. Or, place a polythene bag inside the container and pour the cooled stock into this. When solid, the bag can be removed to leave the dish free again for use.*

To serve: *the stock may be thawed and then added to dishes, or it can be added to soups and sauces in its frozen state.*

TOMATO SOUP

Serves 6

I like to make this soup with those little tomatoes you get when you grow your own, as it is a perfect way to use them up.

2 oz (50 g) butter
2 onions, chopped
2 oz (50 g) flour
1½ pints (900 ml) chicken or vegetable stock
2 lb (900 g) tomatoes, chopped roughly
salt and pepper
oregano, to taste
tabasco sauce, to taste
1 level tablespoon tomato purée

Melt the butter in a large saucepan, add the onions and cook for 5 minutes until a golden brown. Stir in the flour and cook for a minute until a smooth texture, add the stock and bring to the boil, stirring until thickened.

Add the tomatoes, seasoning, oregano, tabasco and tomato purée and bring back to the boil; then reduce the heat, cover with a lid and simmer for about 30 minutes.

Liquidise or blend the soup, pour into a large bowl and cool quickly.

To freeze: *place in a container, cover, label and freeze.*

To serve: *either place in a large saucepan and heat through over a low heat until the soup has thawed, or leave to thaw at room temperature for about 5 hours before reheating. Bring to the boil, stirring, then taste and check the seasoning. Serve with croûtons (page 24).*
Microwave: *defrost 15 minutes and stand 3–5 minutes; reheat 8 minutes and stand 5 minutes.*

COUNTRY VEGETABLE SOUP

Serves 6

This is a colourful soup, and can be made with any combination of root vegetables that you have to hand. It is worth using a really good stock for this soup – ham or bacon stock is perfect.

1½ lb (675 g) mixed root vegetables, diced finely
2 pints (1.2 litres) stock
1 bay leaf
a good pinch of mixed dried herbs
salt and pepper
2 tablespoons tomato purée

🍴 *4 oz (100 g) cooked ham or bacon, diced finely*
¼ pint (150 ml) milk

Put the vegetables, stock, bay leaf, herbs, seasoning and purée in a saucepan and bring to the boil. Cover the pan and simmer for 25 minutes or until the vegetables are tender.

Taste to check the seasoning, remove the bay leaf and cool quickly.

To freeze: *turn into a rigid container, cover, label and freeze.*
🍴 ***To serve:*** *leave to thaw at room temperature for 5 hours, turn into a saucepan and bring to the boil, stirring. Add the ham or bacon, and taste to check the seasoning. Just before serving, remove the pan from the heat and add the milk.*
Microwave: *defrost 15 minutes and stand 3–5 minutes; reheat 6–8 minutes and stand 5 minutes.*

Leek Soup; Tomato Soup; Country Vegetable Soup

LEEK SOUP

Serves 6

This soup is very good served hot or cold.

1½ lb (675 g) leeks
1 large potato
1 oz (25 g) butter
1½ pints (900 ml) chicken stock
salt and freshly ground black pepper

¼ pint (150 ml) single cream
chopped chives

Trim the tops of the leeks to about 1 inch (2.5 cm) above the white parts. Cut the leeks lengthways through the centre and wash well in cold water. Shred finely. Peel and dice the potato.

Heat the butter slowly in a saucepan and add the leeks, then cover and cook slowly over a moderate heat for 15 minutes until soft but not brown. Add the stock and potato, season well and cook for a further 30 minutes. Cool slightly, then purée in a blender or processor. Cool.

To freeze: *turn into a rigid container, cover, label and freeze.*
To serve: *leave to thaw overnight in the refrigerator.*

If serving hot, turn into a saucepan and bring to the boil, stirring, then taste and check the seasoning. Remove the pan from the heat, stir in the cream and turn into a warm dish. Sprinkle with the chives.

If serving the soup cold, taste to check the seasoning and stir in the cream, then turn into a cold dish and sprinkle with the chopped chives.

Microwave: *defrost 15 minutes and stand 3–5 minutes; reheat 6–8 minutes and stand 5 minutes.*

CROÛTONS

I like to make at least half a loaf at a time and then divide them into small bags and freeze. They keep very well in the freezer and give soups that little extra touch when serving.

Remove the crusts from day-old slices of white bread and cut into neat dice. Do not make them too big, as several should fit in a soup spoon – it is best if the bread is about ¼ inch (5 mm) thick.

Fry in shallow or deep fat until a pale golden brown, lift out with a slotted spoon and drain on kitchen paper.

To freeze: *pack in polythene bags, seal and label.*
To serve: *take from the freezer, place in a small dish and reheat in the oven for about 5 minutes at 400°F/200°C/Gas Mark 6 before serving.*

PRAWN COCKTAIL

(Pictured on page 15)
Serves 6
It is handy to keep prawns in the deep freeze and this is a very popular way of serving them. (Do not refreeze once made up as the mayonnaise will curdle.)

8 oz (225 g) frozen prawns
¼ pint (150 ml) mayonnaise
1 tablespoon tomato ketchup
a good pinch of caster sugar
1 tablespoon lemon juice
salt and pepper
a little shredded lettuce

Remove the prawns from their bag and leave to defrost for about 4 hours in the refrigerator (or for 3–4 minutes in the microwave), then drain very well and lay the prawns on kitchen paper towelling to make sure that all the excess water has been absorbed.

Place all the remaining ingredients except the lettuce together in a bowl and mix very well. Taste and check the seasoning.

Put a little shredded lettuce in the bases of six glasses or individual dishes.

Stir the prawns into the sauce and then divide the mixture between the glasses. Serve with thin brown bread and butter and a wedge of lemon.

SMOOTH CHICKEN PÂTÉ

Serves 6–8

This makes a delicious first course served with hot toast and butter.

1 onion, peeled and quartered
12 oz (350 g) chicken livers
4 oz (100 g) sausagemeat
1 heaped tablespoon chopped mixed herbs
salt and freshly ground black pepper
2 tablespoons red wine
approx. 6 rashers of streaky bacon

Heat the oven to 325°F/170°C/Gas Mark 3.

Put the onion with the chicken livers in a processor or blender and reduce to a purée. Add the sausagemeat, herbs, seasoning and wine and process for another minute to blend.

Remove the rind from the bacon rashers and use them to line the bottom and sides of a 1 lb (450 g) loaf tin or dish. Turn in the chicken liver mixture and cover the tin with a piece of foil.

Place the tin in a roasting tin half filled with hot water and cook in the oven for 1½ hours. The pâté is cooked if the juices run clear when the centre is pierced with a skewer and it has shrunk slightly from the sides of the tin.

Place a piece of foil-covered wood on top of the pâté and lightly weight with weights or tins. Leave to become quite cold.

To freeze: *cover with foil, label and freeze or else turn the pâté out, wrap in foil, place in a polythene bag and then seal and label.*
To serve: *unwrap and place on a serving dish and leave to thaw at room temperature for about 6 hours.*
Microwave: *defrost 10-15 minutes and stand 3 minutes.*

Smooth Chicken Pâté; Melon Refresher; Avocado Dip

AVOCADO DIP

Serves 4

I like to serve a dip for a first course if there are just a few guests. Place in the centre of a large plate and arrange small pieces of raw vegetables such as carrots, cucumber, celery, peppers, cauliflower and radishes around it.

2 ripe avocados
2 oz (50 g) cream cheese
4 tablespoons double cream
1 tablespoon mayonnaise
1 tablespoon lemon juice
a little salt and freshly ground black pepper

Cut the avocados in half lengthways, remove the stones, scoop out the flesh into a bowl and mash well with a fork until smooth.

Put the cream cheese in a bowl with the cream and beat well. Stir in the mayonnaise and lemon juice and then add the avocado, mixing well and seasoning to taste.

To freeze: *place in a small plastic container, cover, label and freeze.*
To serve: *leave to thaw at room temperature for 3–4 hours, then turn into a small serving dish.*
Microwave: *defrost 5–7 minutes and stand 2 minutes.*

MELON REFRESHER

Serves 4–6

This is a lovely light starter to a meal, particularly if the main course is rich.

1 honeydew melon
2 tablespoons lemon juice
6 tablespoons white wine
a little caster sugar

lemon twists and lemon balm or mint, to garnish

Halve the melon and remove all the seeds, then peel the melon halves and cut the flesh into neat cubes, using a stainless steel knife.

Place in a plastic container, pour over the lemon juice and wine and sprinkle with a little sugar. Stir to blend. Leave to stand in the refrigerator for about 1 hour for the flavours to blend.

To freeze: *cover, label and freeze.*
🍴 ***To serve:*** *leave to thaw overnight in the refrigerator or for about 8 hours at room temperature. Divide between individual glasses and serve, each garnished with a lemon twist and a small sprig of lemon balm or mint.*
Microwave: *defrost 4–5 minutes and stand 2 minutes.*

SALMON CREAM

Serves 8

This can be made in small dishes, but I find that on the whole it freezes better when made in a large dish or mould. It is very good served for a light lunch with a green salad and granary rolls.

½ oz (15 g) butter
1 level tablespoon flour
¼ pint (150 ml) milk
8 oz (225 g) can of red salmon
½ oz (15 g) packet of powdered gelatine
1 tablespoon lemon juice
salt and pepper
¼ pint (150 ml) mayonnaise
¼ pint (150 ml) double cream

🍴 *cucumber slices and tomato pieces, to garnish*

Melt the butter in a small saucepan, stir in the flour and cook for a minute until a smooth texture. Add the milk and bring to the boil, stirring until the sauce thickens.

Drain the liquor from the salmon into a small bowl, add the gelatine and leave to soak for about 3 minutes.

Remove the sauce from the heat and stir in the gelatine until it has dissolved. Add the lemon juice and season well.

Remove the bones and any pieces of black skin from the salmon and place in a processor or blender with the sauce and the mayonnaise. Process until smooth.

Whisk the cream until it forms soft peaks and fold into the salmon mixture.

Turn into a 1½-pint (900 ml) mould or straight-sided dish and smooth the top. Leave to set in the refrigerator.

To freeze: *cover with a double thickness of foil, label and freeze.*
To serve: *leave to thaw overnight in the refrigerator. Decorate the top of the dish with slices of cucumber and pieces of tomato or, for the mould, turn out on a serving dish and decorate.*
Microwave: *defrost 5–6 minutes (checking after 2–3 minutes) and stand 3 minutes.*

SCALLOPS IN SHELLS

Serves 6

Ask your fishmonger for six deep shells for this dish when you buy the scallops. They are perfect for the recipe and will store well in the freezer.

6 scallops
¼ pint (150 ml) dry cider
1½ oz (40 g) butter
1½ oz (40 g) flour
½ pint (300 ml) milk
salt and pepper
1½ lb (675 g) potatoes, mashed
1 oz (25 g) Cheddar cheese, grated
1 oz (25 g) breadcrumbs, browned

Remove the scallops from their shells, wash thoroughly and remove the black threads. Place in a saucepan with

Scallops in Shells; Taramasalata; Salmon Cream

the cider and then bring to the boil and simmer for 6 minutes. Lift out with a slotted spoon and reserve the cooking liquor. Cut the scallops in slices.

Melt the butter in a saucepan, add the flour and cook for a minute until a smooth texture. Stir in the cooking liquor and milk and bring to the boil, stirring. Season well. Add the sliced scallops.

Pipe the mashed potato in a border around the edge of the six scallop shells. Spoon the sauce into the middle of each.

Mix the cheese with the breadcrumbs and sprinkle over the top of each dish.

To freeze: *open-freeze, pack in polythene bags, seal, label and return to the freezer.*
To serve: *remove from the freezer, take out of the bags and either thaw in the refrigerator overnight or for about 8 hours at room temperature. Cook in a hot oven, 425°F/220°C/Gas Mark 7, for about 25–30 minutes.*

Alternatively, they may be put straight in the hot oven while still frozen and cooked for about 45–50 minutes.
Microwave: *defrost two at a time for 4–6 minutes and stand 2 minutes.*

TARAMASALATA

Serves 4

This is a Greek dish and is delicious served with hot pitta bread, but it can also be served with hot buttered toast or french bread.

8 oz (225 g) smoked cod's roe
2 small slices of white bread
2 tablespoons milk
scant ¼ pint (150 ml) corn oil
2 tablespoons lemon juice
freshly ground black pepper
a little salt if necessary

Remove the skin from the cod's roe and purée in a blender or processor until smooth.

Cut the crusts from the bread and soak the bread in the milk for about 5 minutes. Squeeze out any excess milk and add to the blender.

Add the oil very slowly to the blender, about a teaspoon at a time, puréeing until all has been absorbed. Finally, blend in the lemon juice and black pepper and add salt to taste.

To freeze: *turn into a small strong dish or foil container, cover, label and freeze.*
To serve: *leave to thaw overnight in the refrigerator.*
Microwave: *defrost 4–5 minutes and stand 2 minutes.*

SMOKED SALMON PÂTÉ

Serves 4

Use smoked salmon pieces for this recipe, if you can get them. Often fish shops will let you have the last cuts and small pieces from a side at a very reasonable price.

4 oz (100 g) smoked salmon
3 oz (75 g) butter, melted
2 oz (50 g) cream cheese
1 tablespoon lemon juice
freshly ground black pepper

Put the salmon, 2 oz (50 g) of the butter, cream cheese and lemon juice in a blender or processor and process until smooth. Add pepper to taste.

Turn into a small dish or container, smooth the top and then pour over the remaining melted butter for topping. Place in the refrigerator until firm.

To freeze: *cover with foil, label and freeze.*
To serve: *leave to thaw in the refrigerator overnight and then leave at room temperature for about 1 hour before serving. Serve with brown bread and butter.*
Microwave: *defrost 5–6 minutes and stand 3 minutes.*

Family Meals

Most casseroles are best if thawed completely before reheating – either do this overnight in the refrigerator or take out of the freezer at breakfast time to be ready for the evening meal. Allow the dishes to thaw gently in their packing until they have returned to the same state in which you put them in the freezer. Of course, if you have one, a microwave oven is ideal for thawing and reheating.

If necessary, turn the dish into an ovenproof container and reheat for the time given in the recipe. Always taste and check the seasoning before putting on the table, and also the consistency of the sauce, as it is sometimes necessary to add a little extra stock.

Most prepared dishes are best kept for no longer than 3 months to retain a good flavour. Food with garlic in should not be kept so long, as the flavour will change.

BEEF OLIVES

(Pictured on page 15)

Serves 4

Most butchers are happy to cut you slices of beef for this recipe, and, if they are not too busy, will often beat them out as well.

4 slices of silverside or topside of beef, weighing about 4 oz (100 g) each

For the stuffing
1 oz (25 g) butter
1 onion, chopped
2 rashers of streaky bacon, chopped
2 oz (50 g) mushrooms, chopped
2 oz (50 g) fresh white breadcrumbs
1 tablespoon chopped fresh parsley
1 egg, beaten
salt and pepper

For the sauce
1½ oz (40 g) dripping
1½ oz (40 g) flour
¾ pint (450 ml) beef stock
1 tablespoon tomato purée
8 oz (225 g) carrots, cut in strips
salt and pepper

Trim any fat from the meat. Place each slice in turn between wet greaseproof paper and beat flat with a rolling pin.

Now prepare the stuffing: melt the butter in a small saucepan, add the onion and bacon, cover and cook for 5 minutes. Add the mushrooms and cook for a further 2 minutes. Remove the pan from the heat and add the remaining stuffing ingredients, mixing well. Divide into four equal parts and place a portion on each slice of meat, then roll up and tie neatly with thin string or secure with cocktail sticks.

Melt the dripping for the sauce in a large pan and fry the beef olives all over until brown, then lift out and place on a plate. Stir the flour into the dripping in the pan and cook for a minute until a smooth texture. Add the stock and tomato purée and bring to the boil, stirring. Add the carrots, season well and lay the beef olives on top. Cover and simmer gently for 1 hour. Cool quickly.

To freeze: *turn into a container, cover, label and freeze.*
To serve: *leave to thaw at room temperature for about 6 hours or overnight in the refrigerator. Turn into a saucepan and reheat until boiling. Turn into a dish and serve.*
Microwave: *defrost 20 minutes and stand 20 minutes; reheat 8-10 minutes and stand 5 minutes.*

PORK CASSEROLE WITH CREAM AND MUSHROOMS

Serves 4–6

This is a tasty spiced pork casserole, ideal for an informal party.

1 oz (25 g) flour
salt and pepper
2 teaspoons ground ginger
1½ lb (675 g) casserole or pie pork, cubed
1 tablespoon bacon fat or dripping

For the sauce
¼ teaspoon tabasco sauce
14 oz (397 g) can of tomatoes
6 oz (175 g) button mushrooms
1 tablespoon Worcestershire sauce
2 level tablespoons dark brown sugar
2 tablespoons vinegar
2 cloves of garlic, crushed

5 fl oz (150 ml) carton of soured cream

Heat the oven to 325°F/170°C/Gas Mark 3.

Mix the flour, seasoning and ginger together and use to coat the pork.

Heat the bacon fat or dripping in a large frying pan and fry the pork quickly until browned, turning frequently. Lift out with a slotted spoon and place in a 2½-pint (1.5-litre) ovenproof casserole.

Combine all the ingredients for the sauce and pour over the pork. Cover the dish and cook in the preheated oven for about 2 hours until the meat is tender. Remove the bay leaf and leave to cool.

To freeze: *turn into a rigid container, cover, label and freeze.*
To serve: *leave to thaw overnight in the refrigerator, turn into a large saucepan and bring to the boil, stirring occasionally. Taste to check the seasoning, turn into a hot serving dish and stir in the soured cream.*
Microwave: *defrost 15–20 minutes and stand; reheat 8–10 minutes and stand 5 minutes.*

PORK CHOPS IN CHEESE AND PINEAPPLE SAUCE

Serves 6

This is an unusual way of serving pork chops.

6 pork chops
2 tablespoons oil

For the sauce
1½ oz (40 g) butter
1½ oz (40 g) flour
¾ pint (450 ml) milk
15½ oz (439 g) can of pineapple chunks, drained
4 oz (100 g) well-flavoured Cheddar cheese
1 teaspoon Dijon mustard
salt and pepper

Heat the oven to 400°F/200°C/Gas Mark 6.

Trim any excess fat from the pork. Heat the oil in a large frying pan, add the pork and fry until browned on both sides. Lift out and place in a single layer in an ovenproof dish.

For the sauce: melt the butter in a saucepan, add the flour and cook for a minute. Add the milk and bring to the boil, stirring. Remove from the heat and stir in the pineapple and half of the cheese with the mustard and seasoning.

Pour over the pork chops, cover loosely with foil and cook in the preheated oven for about 30 minutes or until tender.

To freeze: *cool, sprinkle with the remaining cheese, cover, label and freeze.*
To serve: *leave to thaw overnight in the refrigerator, and then place in the oven at 400°F/200°C/Gas Mark 6 for about 30 minutes, until it is hot through and the cheese has melted and browned.*
Microwave: *defrost 15 minutes and stand 3–5 minutes; reheat 6–8 minutes and stand 5 minutes.*

STUFFED GREEN PEPPERS

Serves 4

Buy large peppers when they are cheap and freeze them like this. Serve with slices of warm french bread or granary rolls.

1 onion, chopped
1 carrot, grated
12 oz (350 g) minced beef
1 oz (25 g) flour
½ pint (300 ml) beef stock
salt and pepper
2 large green peppers

For the cheese sauce
1 oz (25 g) butter
1 oz (25 g) flour
½ pint (300 ml) milk
2 oz (50 g) Cheddar cheese, grated
1 teaspoon made mustard
salt and pepper

Put the onion, carrot and mince in a non-stick pan and fry gently to let the fat run out and brown the meat, about 5 minutes. Stir in the flour and cook for a minute. Add the stock and seasoning, cover the pan and simmer for 30 minutes.

Meanwhile, halve the peppers lengthways and remove the seeds and any white pith. Drop the peppers in a pan of boiling water for just 5 minutes, then drain well and place in a foil container or a strong glass dish. Fill with the meat mixture.

Make the sauce: melt the butter in a saucepan, stir in the flour and cook for a minute until a smooth texture. Add the milk and bring to the boil, stirring until thickened. Stir in the cheese, mustard and seasoning. Spoon the sauce over the green peppers and cool quickly.

To freeze: *cover, label and freeze.*

Steak and Kidney Casserole; Stuffed Green Peppers

To serve: *thaw at room temperature for about 7 hours, then place in a moderate oven, 350°F/180°C/Gas Mark 4, for about 40 minutes or until piping hot.*
Microwave: *defrost 10–15 minutes and stand 10 minutes; reheat 5–6 minutes and stand 3 minutes.*

STEAK AND KIDNEY CASSEROLE

Serves 4

Always very popular in our house, I like to put a little smoked bacon in this to give a different flavour, but use unsmoked bacon if you prefer.

1 lb (450 g) stewing steak
8 oz (225 g) ox kidney
1 oz (25 g) flour
1 oz (25 g) dripping
1 large onion, chopped
4 oz (100 g) streaky bacon, chopped in strips
½ pint (300 ml) beef stock
1 teaspoon Worcestershire sauce
1 tablespoon tomato ketchup
salt and pepper
1 bay leaf

Cut the stewing steak into 1-inch (2.5 cm) cubes and cut the kidney into neat pieces, removing the core. Place in a plastic bag with the flour and toss until well coated.

Melt the dripping in a saucepan, add the steak, kidney, onion and bacon and fry quickly for 3–4 minutes. Stir in any flour left in the bag and then add the remaining ingredients. Bring to the boil, stirring, and simmer covered for about 2 hours or until the beef is tender.

Remove from the heat, lift out the bay leaf and taste to check the seasoning. Leave to cool.

To freeze: *turn into a container, cover, label and freeze.*
To serve: *leave to thaw overnight in the refrigerator and then reheat in a saucepan until boiling.*
Microwave: *defrost 20 minutes and stand 20 minutes; reheat 6–8 minutes and stand 5 minutes.*

LAMB CURRY

Serves 6

This is a really good lamb curry – serve it with plenty of plain boiled rice.

2 oz (50 g) butter
2 lb (900 g) lamb fillet, cubed
2 onions, chopped finely
1-inch (2.5 cm) piece of fresh root ginger, peeled and cubed
2 cloves of garlic, peeled
2 green chillies
2 oz (50 g) unsalted cashew nuts
¼ teaspoon ground cloves
¼ teaspoon ground cardamom
2 teaspoons ground coriander
¼ teaspoon ground turmeric
6 tablespoons water
½ pint (300 ml) natural yogurt
1 tablespoon lemon juice
salt and pepper

Melt the butter in a saucepan, add the lamb and onions and fry for 5 minutes.

Put the ginger, garlic, chillies, nuts and all the spices with the water in a blender or processor and purée until smooth. Stir into the meat mixture with the yogurt and mix well, then cover the pan and simmer for 1 hour.

Stir in the lemon juice and continue cooking for a further hour or until the lamb is tender. Taste and check the seasoning. Cool.

To freeze: *turn into a rigid container, cover, label and freeze. Do not store for too long (about 1–2 weeks).*
To serve: *leave to thaw overnight in the refrigerator, then turn into a saucepan and bring to the boil. Taste to check the seasoning before serving.*
Microwave: *defrost 15 minutes and stand; reheat 6–8 minutes and stand 3 minutes.*

SAVOURY MEATBALLS

Serves 4–6

I like to serve these with a dish of noodles and a crisp green salad.

8 oz (225 g) beef sausagemeat
8 oz (225 g) minced beef
salt and pepper
1 oz (25 g) flour, plus extra for flouring
1 tablespoon oil
1 onion, chopped
1 green pepper, deseeded and chopped
¾ pint (450 ml) beef stock
2 tablespoons tomato purée
4 oz (100 g) mushrooms, sliced

Put the sausagemeat and minced beef in a bowl with seasoning and work together until evenly blended. Lightly flour your hands and roll the mixture into 24 smooth balls and then coat these in the flour.

Heat the oil in a large saucepan, add the meatballs and onion and fry quickly to brown all over. Drain off any excess fat, sprinkle in any spare flour and then add the green pepper, stock and tomato purée. Bring to the boil, stirring, and season well. Partially cover the pan and simmer for 20 minutes, then add the mushrooms and continue cooking for a further 10 minutes. Taste and check the seasoning.

To freeze: *leave to become quite cold, turn into a container, cover, label and freeze.*
To serve: *leave to thaw overnight in the refrigerator or for about 7–8 hours at room temperature. Turn into a saucepan and reheat carefully, bring to the boil and simmer for a few minutes to make sure that the meatballs are hot through.*
Microwave: *defrost 10-12 minutes and stand 5 minutes; reheat 5-6 minutes and stand 3 minutes.*

Beefburgers; Savoury Meatballs; Beef Pasties

BEEF PASTIES
Makes 4

I find these are very handy to have in the freezer; in winter they can be served with gravy and vegetables and in summer they can be served with salad or taken on a picnic and eaten with your fingers.

For the pastry
8 oz (225 g) plain flour
2 oz (50 g) margarine
2 oz (50 g) lard
approx. 3 tablespoons cold water
a little milk, to glaze

For the filling
8 oz (225 g) lean chuck or rib steak
1 carrot, chopped finely
1 onion, chopped finely
1 medium-size potato, diced finely
¼ teaspoon mixed dried herbs
salt and pepper
3 tablespoons beef stock or gravy

First prepare the pastry: put the flour in a bowl, add the fats (cut in small pieces) and rub in with the fingertips until the mixture resembles breadcrumbs. Mix to a firm dough with the cold water. Leave in the refrigerator while you make the filling.

Trim any fat from the meat and cut into small pieces (if you have a food processor, use this to cut up the meat as it saves a lot of time). Put in a bowl with all the other filling ingredients and mix well.

Heat the oven to 400°F/200°C/Gas Mark 6.

Divide the pastry into four equal pieces and roll out each piece to a circle 7 inches (18 cm) in diameter (use a small plate to get a good shape).

Divide the filling between the pastry circles. Dampen the edges of the pastry and then fold together over the filling. Seal firmly and crimp the edges or mark with a fork.

Put on a baking tray and brush with a little milk to glaze. Bake in the oven for about 50–60 minutes or until the pastry is a golden brown and the meat is tender. Cool quickly.

To freeze: *carefully wrap in foil or lay in a single layer in a rigid container. Cover, label and freeze. Cooked pastry is fragile and so great care needs to be taken when packing for the freezer.*
To serve: *leave to thaw at room temperature for about 6 hours and then place on a baking tray and heat through in the oven at 350°F/180°C/Gas Mark 4 for about 20 minutes.*
Microwave: *defrost two at a time for 5–7 minutes and stand 5 minutes; reheat 2–4 minutes and stand 3 minutes.*

BEEFBURGERS

Makes 8

I like to make my own beefburgers and keep them ready in the deep freeze.

1 lb (450 g) minced beef
8 oz (225 g) beef sausagemeat
salt
1 tablespoon fresh chopped mixed herbs
¼ teaspoon cayenne pepper
a little flour

Place all the ingredients except the flour in a bowl and mix thoroughly until evenly blended.

Divide the mixture into eight equal-sized pieces and with lightly floured hands shape each piece into a burger about 3 inches (7.5 cm) in diameter.

To freeze: *freeze uncooked: interleave with greaseproof paper, wrap in foil and label, or store in a container.*
To serve: *cook straight from frozen. Either grill or fry for about 15–20 minutes, turning during cooking.*
Microwave: *cook on High 2-3 minutes and stand 3 minutes.*

ROAST STUFFED SHOULDER OF LAMB

Serves 8–10

This is perfect for the busy hostess: prepare not more than 1 week ahead and then place ready in the freezer! Be sure to use lamb that has not already been frozen.

1 small shoulder of lamb, boned
1½ oz (40 g) butter
1 onion, chopped
4 oz (100 g) mushrooms, chopped
4 oz (100 g) chicken livers, chopped
4 oz (100 g) fresh white or brown breadcrumbs
2 tablespoons chopped parsley
1 teaspoon grated lemon rind
a little dried thyme
1 egg, beaten
salt and pepper

First open out the shoulder of lamb and remove any large pieces of fat.

Now make the stuffing: melt the butter in a small saucepan, add the onion, cover and cook gently for about 10 minutes so that it is soft but not brown. Add the mushrooms and chopped liver and cook for 3 minutes, then remove the pan from the heat, stir in the remaining ingredients and mix well. Cool, spoon into the lamb shoulder and reshape it, securing with string if necessary.

To freeze: *place in a large plastic bag, label and freeze.*
To serve: *leave to thaw in the refrigerator for about 24 hours. Weigh the joint and calculate the cooking time, allowing 30 minutes to the lb (450 g), plus 30 minutes. Heat the oven to 375°F/190°C/Gas Mark 5. Place the lamb in a roasting tin and roast in the oven until tender – the juices of the meat will run clear when pricked with a skewer. Place on a serving dish and serve with gravy, mint sauce and redcurrant jelly.*

Roast Stuffed Shoulder of Lamb; Lamb Navarin

Microwave: *defrost 8–10 minutes and stand 20 minutes per lb (450 g); reheat on Cook (Level 7/80%) 8 minutes and stand 15 minutes per lb (450 g).*

LAMB NAVARIN

Serves 4

'Navarin' is a French term for a casserole that is full of lamb and young vegetables and a main meal in itself. It is perfect to leave cooking for the family while you are out.

8 small lean lamb chops or pieces of middle neck
1 oz (25 g) flour
1 oz (25 g) dripping
½ pint (300 ml) beef stock
14 oz (397 g) can of tomatoes
8 oz (225 g) carrots, halved and then quartered lengthways
8 oz (225 g) small whole or pickling onions
salt and pepper
1 lb (450 g) small new potatoes, scraped

8 oz (225 g) peas or broad beans

Heat the oven to 325°F/170°C/Gas Mark 3.

Trim any excess fat from the lamb and coat the meat in the flour. Heat the dripping in a large frying pan and quickly fry the meat to brown on both sides. Lift out and place in a large 4½-pint (2.5-litre) casserole.

Drain off any fat remaining in the pan, put in the stock and tomatoes and bring to the boil.

Add the carrots and the onions to the casserole. Pour the tomato sauce over the meat and season well. Cover with a lid and cook in the oven for about 1 hour.

Add the potatoes, ensuring that they are well pushed down into the sauce, and return to the oven for a further 45 minutes or until the meat and vegetables are cooked. Taste and check the seasoning and cool quickly.

To freeze: *turn into a large container, cover, label and freeze.*
To serve: *leave to thaw overnight in the refrigerator, then turn into the large casserole it was cooked in. Add the peas*

or broad beans and heat through in a moderate oven (350°F/ 180°C/Gas Mark 4) for about 45 minutes or until it is hot through, the sauce boiling and the peas or beans tender.
Microwave: *defrost 20 minutes and stand 10 minutes; reheat 8–10 minutes and stand 5 minutes.*

FRENCH-STYLE PORK

Serves 4

I like to serve this with chunks of hot french bread.

1 green pepper
1 red pepper
2 tablespoons sunflower oil
2 onions, sliced
1 clove of garlic, crushed
4 pork chops
1 lb (450 g) courgettes, sliced
1 lb (450 g) tomatoes, peeled and quartered
salt and pepper

Remove the seeds and white pith from the peppers and cut them into strips.

Heat the oil in a large saucepan and add the peppers, onions and garlic. Cover with a lid and cook slowly for 15 minutes, stirring occasionally, until the vegetables are soft but not brown.

Meanwhile, remove the skin and any fat from the chops, place them in a frying pan over a gentle heat to allow the fat to run out, then fry for 10 minutes, turning once, until they are brown on both sides.

Add the courgettes, tomatoes and seasoning to the saucepan and lay the pork chops on top. Cook partially covered for about 20 minutes until the pork is tender and the vegetables soft, then taste and check the seasoning. Cool quickly.

To freeze: *turn into a container, cover, label and freeze.*
To serve: *leave to thaw overnight in the refrigerator. Turn into a saucepan and reheat gently until boiling. Taste to check the seasoning and spoon into a warm serving dish.*

Microwave: *defrost 15–20 minutes and stand 10 minutes; reheat 6–8 minutes and stand 5 minutes.*

SWEET AND SOUR PORK CASSEROLE

Serves 4–6

Serve this dish with either plain boiled noodles or rice.

1½ lb (675 g) casserole or pie pork
2 tablespoons sunflower oil
2 onions, chopped
15 oz (425 g) can of pineapple pieces
3 tablespoons vinegar
2 oz (50 g) soft brown sugar
2 rounded tablespoons tomato purée
salt and pepper
1 large green pepper, deseeded and sliced

2 level tablespoons cornflour

Trim any pieces of fat from the meat and cube. Heat the oil in a saucepan and fry the meat and onions for 3–5 minutes. Drain off any excess oil and fat.

Drain the juice from the pineapple pieces and make up to ½ pint (300 ml) with water, stir this into the pan with the vinegar, brown sugar, purée and seasoning and bring to the boil, stirring. Cover the pan and simmer for about 1 hour and then stir in the pineapple pieces and green pepper and cook for a further 15 minutes or until the pork is tender. Cool quickly.

To freeze: *turn into a container, cover, label and freeze.*
To serve: *leave to thaw overnight in the refrigerator, then turn into a saucepan and bring to the boil, stirring. Blend the cornflour with a little cold water, add a spoonful of the hot sauce to blend and then stir into the saucepan and cook for a minute until thickened. Taste and check the seasoning. Serve.*
Microwave: *defrost 20 minutes and stand 10 minutes; reheat 8 minutes and stand 5 minutes.*

Sweet and Sour Pork Casserole; French-style Pork

KIDNEYS IN SHERRY SAUCE

Serves 4

I like to serve these with buttered noodles and a crisp green vegetable such as broccoli.

12 lamb's kidneys
4 rashers of streaky bacon
1½ oz (40 g) butter
1 onion, sliced
2 oz (50 g) flour
½ pint (300 ml) beef stock
3 tablespoons sherry
1 tablespoon tomato purée
salt and pepper

🍴 *4 oz (100 g) button mushrooms, quartered*

Cut the kidneys in half horizontally, remove the skins and cores and cut each half in two or three pieces. Remove the rind from the bacon and cut into strips.

Melt the butter in a frying pan and add the kidneys, bacon and onion and fry for 5 minutes, stirring. Add the flour and cook for a minute and then stir in the stock, sherry, purée and seasoning and bring to the boil, stirring. Simmer for 5 minutes. Taste to check the seasoning and cool quickly.

To freeze: *turn into a container, cover, label and freeze.*
🍴 ***To serve:*** *leave to thaw at room temperature, about 5 hours, then turn into a saucepan and reheat until it comes to the boil. Add the mushrooms and simmer for 3–4 minutes. Turn into a serving dish.*
Microwave: *defrost 15–20 minutes and stand 10 minutes; reheat 6–8 minutes and stand 5 minutes.*

CHICKEN IN MUSHROOM SAUCE

Serves 4

This casserole is very popular in our house and is handy to keep in the freezer for emergencies.

4 chicken joints or 8 drumsticks, skinned
2 tablespoons fresh chopped mixed herbs
salt and pepper
a large knob of butter
5 tablespoons white wine or sherry

For the sauce
1 oz (25 g) butter
1 oz (25 g) flour
½ pint (300 ml) milk

🍴 *4 oz (100 g) mushrooms, sliced*
chopped fresh herbs (optional)

Heat the oven to 350°F/180°C/Gas Mark 4.

Lay the chicken pieces in a single layer in an ovenproof dish. Sprinkle with the herbs and seasoning, dot with the knob of butter, pour over the wine or sherry and cover the dish with a piece of foil. Bake in the oven for 45 minutes (a little less if using drumsticks).

Meanwhile, make the sauce: melt the butter in a saucepan, stir in the flour and cook for a minute until a smooth texture, then gradually add the milk and bring to the boil, stirring, until the sauce has thickened. Stir in the juices from the chicken and taste to check the seasoning.

To freeze: *lay the chicken pieces in a rigid container, pour over the sauce and leave to cool. Cover, label and freeze.*

🍴 ***To serve:*** *leave to thaw overnight in the refrigerator, then place in an ovenproof dish and reheat in the oven, 350°F/180°C/Gas Mark 4, for about 40 minutes until the chicken is hot through and the sauce is boiling. Add the mushrooms and cook for a further 5 minutes. Add fresh herbs if liked.*

Microwave: *defrost 10–15 minutes and stand 10 minutes; reheat 10 minutes and stand 3–5 minutes.*

CHICKEN PAPRIKA

Serves 4–5

The sauce in this recipe is also marvellous with leftover cooked chicken. I make up a half quantity of the sauce and freeze it separately in a small container – I find it very handy to have small portions in the freezer, as sometimes there is only one member of the family to feed.

3 lb (1.3 kg) chicken
½ pint (300 ml) dry cider
salt and pepper
1 onion, chopped
4 level teaspoons paprika
1½ oz (40 g) flour
14 oz (397 g) can of tomatoes

🍴 *a little soured cream or yogurt*

Heat the oven to 350°F/180°C/Gas Mark 4.

Place the chicken in a dish, pour over the cider and season well. Cover with a lid or piece of foil and cook in the oven for 1½ hours or until tender. Test the thickest part of the leg with a skewer – if the juices run clear, the chicken is cooked. Lift out the chicken and strain off the cider. Carve the chicken into convenient portions and lay in a rigid container.

Take 3 tablespoons of fat from the top of the chicken stock, place in a saucepan with the onion and cook for 5 minutes until the onion is soft and opaque, then stir in the paprika and flour and cook for a minute. Stir in the cider and the can of tomatoes and bring to the boil, stirring. Simmer for 20 minutes. Taste and check the seasoning. Cool quickly and spoon over the chicken.

To freeze: *cover, label and freeze.*

🍴 ***To serve:*** *thaw overnight in the refrigerator, place in a casserole and reheat in a moderate oven (350°F/180°C/Gas*

Chicken Paprika; Chicken in Mushroom Sauce

Mark 4) for about 50–60 minutes until piping hot. Stir in the soured cream or yogurt just before serving.
***Microwave:** defrost 15–20 minutes and stand 5 minutes; reheat 8–10 minutes and stand 5 minutes.*

FISH CAKES

Serves 4

Use any fish you like for this recipe; even a can of salmon or tuna fish is very good.

8 oz (225 g) cooked flaked fish, e.g. cod, smoked haddock or whiting
12 oz (350 g) potatoes, freshly cooked and mashed
1 tablespoon chopped parsley
salt and pepper
2 eggs, beaten
breadcrumbs, browned

oil for frying

Place the fish, potato, parsley and seasoning in a bowl with one of the beaten eggs and mix thoroughly. Shape the mixture into a roll and cut into eight even-sized slices.

Coat the fish cakes in the other beaten egg and then toss in the browned breadcrumbs.

***To freeze:** open-freeze, pack in a rigid container, cover, label and freeze again.*
***To serve:** thaw at room temperature for 5 minutes, then fry in hot oil for 4–5 minutes on each side until golden brown. Lift out and drain on kitchen paper. Serve with a green vegetable and tomato sauce.*

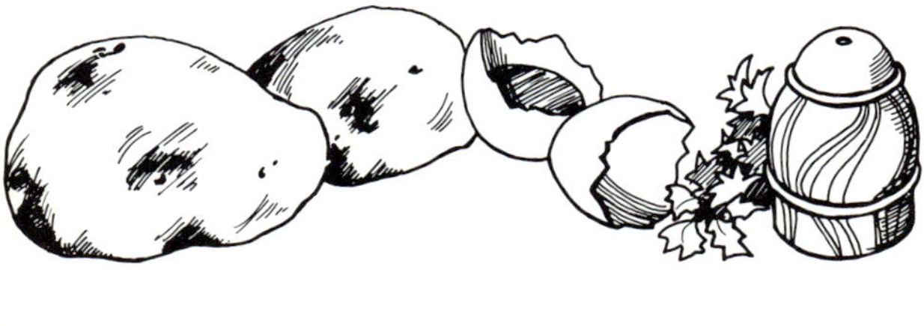

FISH PIE

Serves 6

This is always a great favourite. I vary the fish I use according to the time of year and whichever is the best buy.

8 oz (225 g) white fish
8 oz (225 g) smoked fish
4 oz (100 g) frozen peas
¾ pint (450 ml) milk
1½ oz (40 g) butter
1½ oz (40 g) flour
4 oz (100 g) peeled prawns
2 tablespoons mayonnaise
salt and pepper
1½ lb (675 g) potatoes, mashed

Skin the two pieces of fish, remove any bones and place in a saucepan with the peas and milk. Simmer gently for about 8 minutes or until the fish is cooked and will flake easily with a fork. Strain the milk into a measure and tip the fish and peas into a bowl, lightly breaking up the fish with a fork.

Rinse out the saucepan and melt the butter in it. Add the flour, cook for a minute until a smooth texture, gradually add the milk and bring to the boil, stirring until the sauce has thickened. Add the prawns, mayonnaise, seasoning, fish and peas to the pan and mix together.

Turn into a 3-pint (1.8-litre) foil dish or tough casserole. Leave to cool and then cover with a layer of the mashed potato or pipe a border of it around the edge.

To freeze: *cover, label and freeze.*
To serve: *leave to thaw overnight in the refrigerator and then remove the lid and heat in a hot oven (425°F/220°C/Gas Mark 7) for about 35 minutes until piping hot.*
Microwave: *defrost 10–12 minutes and stand 5 minutes.*

MEDITERRANEAN FISH CASSEROLE

Serves 4–6

This is a delicious way to serve fish for a change. Serve with chunks of french bread. Because it has garlic in, do not keep for too long as the garlic flavour tends to change.

2 tablespoons sunflower oil
1 large onion, chopped
1 clove of garlic, crushed
1 level tablespoon tomato purée
3 medium-size potatoes, peeled and diced
14 oz (397 g) can of tomatoes
1 pint (600 ml) good fish or chicken stock
salt and pepper
a good pinch of sugar
1 lb (450 g) white fish, such as cod or haddock

1 tablespoon chopped fresh parsley

Heat the oil in a large saucepan and fry the onion and garlic for about 5 minutes or until tender. Add the purée, diced potatoes, tomatoes, stock, seasoning and sugar and simmer for about 10 minutes so that the potato cubes are tender.

Meanwhile, remove all the skin and bone from the fish and cut into neat pieces, no bigger than 1 inch (2.5 cm). Add to the pan and simmer for 5 minutes until cooked. Cool quickly.

To freeze: *turn into a rigid container, cover, label and freeze.*
To serve: *thaw at room temperature for 5–6 hours, then turn into a saucepan and bring slowly to the boil. Add the chopped parsley, taste to check the seasoning and turn into a large tureen to serve.*
Microwave: *defrost 20 minutes and stand 10 minutes; reheat 6–8 minutes and stand 3 minutes.*

Fish Cakes; Mediterranean Fish Casserole; Fish Pie

SUMMER VEGETABLES AU GRATIN

Serves 6

Use any combination of vegetables that you have to hand for this recipe. It is good as a meal on its own but can also be served with meat.

8 oz (225 g) new carrots, cut evenly in lengths
1 small cauliflower, broken into florets
8 oz (225 g) french beans, trimmed
4 oz (100 g) fresh peas
2 tablespoons sunflower oil
1 oz (25 g) butter
1 oz (25 g) fresh white or brown breadcrumbs
salt and pepper

For the cheese sauce
2 oz (50 g) butter
2 oz (50 g) flour
¾ pint (450 ml) milk
1 teaspoon made mustard
4 oz (100 g) Cheddar cheese, grated
salt and pepper

Cook the carrots in boiling salted water for 5 minutes. Add the cauliflower and beans and cook for a further 5 minutes, then add the peas and cook for 3 minutes.

Meanwhile, heat the oil and butter in a frying pan and fry the breadcrumbs until golden brown, stirring frequently. Season and take out of the pan.

Drain the vegetables well, reserving ¼ pint (150 ml) cooking water, and place in a large, shallow foil dish.

Make the sauce: melt the butter in a saucepan and stir in the flour. Cook, stirring constantly, for a minute until a smooth texture, then add the milk and reserved cooking water and bring to the boil, stirring. Stir in the mustard and cheese and season to taste. Pour the sauce over the vegetables and sprinkle with the breadcrumbs. Cool.

To freeze: *cover, label and freeze.*
To serve: *this is best thawed overnight in the refrigerator and then placed in a moderate oven (350°F/180°C/Gas Mark 4)*

for 40 minutes until hot through and bubbling.
Microwave: *defrost 15–20 minutes and stand 5 minutes; reheat 5–6 minutes and stand 3 minutes.*

BEANY GOULASH

Serves 4

This is a vegetarian dish, but it is so good that I often serve it with sausages, beefburgers or gammon rashers. It makes a very good meal for hungry teenagers.

8 oz (225 g) dried butter beans
2 tablespoons sunflower oil
2 large onions, sliced
2 level tablespoons flour
1 tablespoon paprika
14 oz (397 g) can of tomatoes
¼ pint (150 ml) vegetable stock or water
1 large green pepper, deseeded and sliced
salt and pepper

Place the butter beans in a bowl, cover with cold water and leave to stand overnight.

Next day, drain well, place in a saucepan, cover with fresh cold water and bring to the boil. Simmer for about 30–45 minutes or until tender – the cooking time will vary with the brand of beans used. Drain well and leave on one side.

Heat the oil in a large saucepan, add the onions and fry for about 5 minutes until tender. Stir in the flour and paprika and cook for a minute. Add all the remaining ingredients and bring to the boil, stirring. Cover the pan and simmer for 10 minutes. Stir in the beans and cook for a further 10 minutes. Cool.

To freeze: *place in a container, cover, label and freeze.*
To serve: *leave to thaw at room temperature for 4–5 hours, then turn into a saucepan and heat through gently, stirring occasionally, until boiling hot. Serve with a green vegetable and granary rolls.*
Microwave: *defrost 15–20 minutes and stand 10 minutes; reheat 6–8 minutes and stand 3–5 minutes.*

NUT ROAST

Serves 4

A nut roast is always a great favourite with vegetarians. It can be served either hot or cold, with a mixed salad or a green vegetable such as broccoli.

4 oz (100 g) dry-roasted peanuts
4 oz (100 g) shelled cashew nuts
2 oz (50 g) butter, plus a little extra for greasing
1 large onion, chopped
1 large tomato, skinned and chopped
2 small eating apples, peeled, cored and diced
1 oz (25 g) rolled oats
1 tablespoon fresh chopped mixed herbs
salt and pepper
1 egg, beaten
a little milk

slices of tomato, to garnish

Heat the oven to 350°F/180°C/Gas Mark 4. Grease a 1 lb (450 g) loaf tin.

Finely chop the nuts. Heat the butter in a saucepan, add the onion, tomato and apples and fry for about 5 minutes to soften. Add the nuts, oats, herbs and seasoning, taking care not to add too much salt. Bind with the beaten egg and just enough milk to give a moist consistency.

Press into the loaf tin, cover with a piece of buttered foil or greaseproof paper and bake in the oven for 1 hour, removing the paper for the last 15 minutes of cooking time. Turn out and leave to cool.

To freeze: *wrap in foil, label and freeze.*
To serve: *leave to thaw at room temperature, about 5 hours, and then heat through in a moderate oven (350°F/180°C/Gas Mark 4) for about 30 minutes, covered with a piece of buttered paper. Garnish with slices of tomato.*
Microwave: *defrost 15–20 minutes and stand 3–5 minutes; reheat 7–8 minutes and stand 3–5 minutes.*

Summer Vegetables au Gratin; Beany Goulash; Nut Roast

Hot and Cold Puddings

Fruit pies, tarts and sponge puddings are an asset to have ready in the freezer, and add a substantial finish to a meal when you have been out all day. Pastry can be very fragile, so wrap and pack with care before storing in the freezer. (Microwave ovens, if you have one, are great for thawing and reheating hot pies and puddings.)

Ice cream is a boon to have in the freezer. It is a perfect accompaniment to many hot dishes, can be used as the basis of a variety of puddings or can be served just on its own with a sauce and a shortbread finger. Always keep one or two flavours.

When soft fruit is in season and most plentiful, I like to make and freeze a number of fruit dishes, such as fools and sauces. Mousses are a great standby, but do not keep these for too long as they tend to go rubbery in texture after freezing.

PEAR CRUMBLE

Serves 4

This is a good way of serving windfall pears. It is lovely served with vanilla ice cream.

1½ lb (675 g) cooking pears, peeled and cored
2 tablespoons golden syrup
grated rind of ½ orange
6 oz (175 g) plain flour
3 oz (75 g) margarine
2 oz (50 g) demerara sugar

Cut the pears into even slices, place in a saucepan, cover with boiling water, bring to the boil and cook for just 2 minutes. Drain very well and place in an ovenproof dish. Using a hot tablespoon, trickle the golden syrup over the pears and sprinkle with the orange rind.

Now make the crumble: place the flour in a bowl, rub

in the margarine with your fingertips until it resembles breadcrumbs and stir in the sugar. Spoon over the pears and press down lightly.

To freeze: *freeze uncovered until firm, cover with a foil lid, label and return to the freezer.*
To serve: *unwrap and cook in the oven at 350°F/180°C/Gas Mark 4 for about 45 minutes.*
Microwave: *defrost 5–6 minutes; reheat 4–5 minutes and brown under grill.*

PINEAPPLE MOUSSE

(Pictured on page 15)
Serves 6
It is better not to keep this too long in the deep freeze, as it can go a little rubbery – about 2–3 weeks is best.

3 eggs, separated
juice of 1 lemon
2 oz (50 g) caster sugar
15 oz (425 g) can of pineapple pieces
¾ oz (20 g) powdered gelatine (1½ packets)
¼ pint (150 ml) double cream

Place the egg yolks in a bowl with the lemon juice and sugar and stand over a pan of simmering water, whisking until the mixture is thick and will leave a trail when the whisk is lifted out. Remove from the heat and leave to cool, whisking occasionally.

Drain 4 tablespoons of syrup from the can of pineapple and place in a small bowl with the gelatine. Leave to stand for 2–3 minutes until it becomes a sponge and then stand over a pan of simmering water and leave until dissolved.

Meanwhile, purée the pineapple pieces and the remaining syrup in a blender or processor.

Remove the gelatine from the heat and stir in the pineapple purée. Add to the egg yolk mixture and leave in a cool place until starting to thicken and just beginning to set. Whisk the egg whites until stiff and then whisk the cream until it forms soft peaks. Fold first the cream and then the egg whites evenly through the pineapple mixture. Turn into a toughened glass container.

To freeze: *cover with a foil lid, label and freeze.*
To serve: *leave to thaw in the refrigerator for about 6 hours. If liked, decorate the top with rosettes of whipped cream or serve with a little single cream poured over the top.*
Microwave: *defrost 1–2 minutes, checking every 30 seconds.*

BASIC ICE CREAM

Serves 8–10

Everybody needs to keep some ice cream in the freezer, whether to serve with hot puddings or a flavoured version to serve on its own or with fruit. This exotic, home-made recipe needs no whisking during freezing, is thick and creamy and just needs to be frozen until solid.

4 eggs, separated
4 oz (100 g) caster sugar
½ pint (300 ml) double cream
a little vanilla essence (optional)

Whisk the egg yolks in a small bowl until blended. In a larger bowl, whisk the egg whites with a hand rotary or electric whisk on high speed until stiff, then whisk in the sugar, a teaspoonful at a time – the whites will get stiffer and stiffer as the sugar is added.

Whisk the cream until it forms soft peaks and then carefully fold it into the meringue mixture with the egg yolks, adding a little vanilla essence if liked.

To freeze: *turn the mixture into a 2½-pint (1.5-litre) container, cover, label and freeze.*
To serve: *leave to thaw at room temperature for 5–10 minutes, then serve in scoops in small dishes or glasses.*

Strawberry Ice Cream with Fresh Strawberry Sauce; Tutti Frutti Pudding

VARIATIONS

Raspberry, strawberry or gooseberry: Stir ¼ pint (150 ml) fruit purée into the ice cream just before freezing, adding a little colouring if liked.
Apricot: Drain a 14 oz (420 g) can of apricots, purée the fruit and stir into the ice cream just before freezing.
Chocolate: Add 4 oz (100 g) melted plain chocolate to the egg yolks in the basic recipe. Use chilled evaporated milk instead of the double cream.
Coffee: Add 3–4 tablespoons of coffee essence to the basic ice cream, adding with the egg yolks.
Lemon: Add the grated rind and juice of 2 lemons to the basic ice cream, adding with the egg yolks.

FRESH STRAWBERRY SAUCE

Makes approx. ½ pint (300 ml)

Fresh strawberries don't freeze well, but puréed ones do, and in the summer I like to make up this sauce and store it in small handy containers in the freezer. It is perfect served with vanilla ice cream or peaches and is very special if served with fresh raspberries.

1 lb (450 g) fresh strawberries
approx. 6 oz (175 g) caster or icing sugar
juice of 1 lemon

Hull but do not wash the strawberries, place them in a blender or processor with the other ingredients and purée until smooth. Taste and check that you have added sufficient sugar for your taste.

To freeze: *turn into a convenient-sized plastic container, cover, label and freeze.*
To serve: *the sauce is best if allowed to thaw overnight in the refrigerator, but it can be left to thaw at room temperature for about 3–4 hours, stirring occasionally.*
Microwave: *defrost 2–3 minutes.*

TUTTI FRUTTI PUDDING

Serves 8–10

This is a rather special pudding which looks quite spectacular when decorated and served.

6 oz (175 g) mixed chopped glacé pineapple, dried apricots, glacé cherries and raisins
4–6 tablespoons sherry, brandy or fresh orange juice
4 eggs, separated
4 oz (100 g) caster sugar
½ pint (300 ml) double cream

½ pint (300 ml) whipping cream, whipped
slivers of toasted almonds

Place the mixed chopped fruit in a small bowl, add the sherry, brandy or juice and stir well. Cover with a piece of cling film and leave to stand overnight. The fruit will plump up and absorb the liquid.

Whisk the egg yolks in a small bowl until blended. In a larger bowl, whisk the egg whites with a hand rotary or electric whisk on high speed until they are stiff, then whisk in the sugar, a teaspoonful at a time – the egg whites will get stiffer and stiffer as the sugar is added.

Whisk the cream until it forms soft peaks and then fold it into the meringue mixture with the egg yolks and fruit. Turn into a 3-pint (1.8-litre) strong glass bowl.

To freeze: *cover with foil, label and freeze.*

To serve: *take from the freezer, leave to stand at room temperature for 5 minutes and then turn out on to a serving dish. Completely cover with the whipped cream and scatter over the almond slivers.*

LEMON CRUNCH

Serves 8

This is a very good pudding to keep in the deep freeze. Perfect for the unexpected guest, it can be served just as it is or with fruit (we like it with raspberries or sliced peaches).

3 oz (75 g) cornflakes, crushed
3 level tablespoons caster sugar
1½ oz (40 g) butter, melted

For the filling
2 eggs, separated
6 oz (196 g) can of condensed milk
grated rind and juice of 1 lemon
3 level tablespoons caster sugar

Place the cornflakes in a bowl with the caster sugar, mix well and then stir in the melted butter until thoroughly blended. Press half this mixture over the base of an 8-inch (20 cm) loose-bottomed cake tin.

For the filling: place the egg yolks in a bowl and beat until creamy, then blend in the condensed milk, lemon rind and juice – the mixture will start to thicken at this stage.

Whisk the egg whites until stiff with a rotary or electric hand whisk and then whisk in the sugar, a teaspoonful at a time. Fold into the lemon mixture and then turn into the cake tin and smooth the top. Cover with the remaining cornflakes, pressing lightly so that they adhere to the mixture.

To freeze: *cover with a double thickness of foil, label and freeze.*
To serve: *leave to stand at room temperature for about 5–10 minutes, then turn out on to a serving dish and serve cut in wedges.*

Raspberry Cream Gâteau;
Individual Orange Mousses; Lemon Crunch

INDIVIDUAL ORANGE MOUSSES

Makes 6 small mousses

I find it very handy to have small mousses in the deep freeze. They thaw quickly and you can take out just the number you want.

3 eggs, separated
4 oz (100 g) caster sugar
grated rind and juice of 2 medium-size oranges
3 level teaspoons powdered gelatine
3 tablespoons cold water
¼ pint (150 ml) double cream

orange segments or cream

Put the egg yolks, sugar, orange rind and juice in a heatproof bowl and stand over a pan of simmering water, whisking the mixture until it is thick and the whisk leaves a trail when lifted out. Remove the pan from the heat and continue whisking for a little longer.

Place the gelatine with the cold water in a small bowl or cup and leave to stand for 3 minutes to form a sponge, then place over a small pan of hot water until dissolved. Remove from the heat, leave to cool slightly and then stir into the orange mixture. Leave in a cool place until beginning to set.

Meanwhile, whisk the cream until thick, whisk the egg whites until stiff and fold both into the orange mixture.

Divide the mixture between individual strong glass or ramekin dishes, or if you don't have these, use empty yogurt or cream cartons.

To freeze: *cover with foil lids, label and freeze.*
To serve: *turn out on individual plates and leave to thaw at room temperature for about 45 minutes. Decorate with orange segments or swirls of cream.*
Microwave: *defrost 1 minute, checking after 30 seconds.*

RASPBERRY CREAM GÂTEAU

Serves 8

This is a very good way to make the first of the raspberries go quite a long way. I like to serve the gâteau decorated with a little extra cream and raspberries or with a bowl of Fresh Strawberry Sauce (page 68).

two 7-inch (18 cm) victoria sandwich cakes
¼ pint (150 ml) double cream
a little caster sugar
a few drops of vanilla essence
a good 4 oz (100 g) fresh raspberries

Lay the cakes flat on the table.

Whisk the double cream until it forms soft peaks and then whisk in a little caster sugar and a few drops of vanilla essence to taste. Spread this mixture over one of the cakes, cover with a thick layer of raspberries and press on the remaining cake.

To freeze: *wrap in a double thickness of foil, place in a polythene bag, label and freeze.*
To serve: *unwrap the cake and place on a serving dish. Leave to thaw in the refrigerator for 6 hours and then at room temperature for 2 hours.*
Microwave: *defrost 2–3 minutes, checking after each minute.*

CHOCOLATE AND PEAR UPSIDE-DOWN PUDDING

Serves 6–8

This is a good filling pudding to serve when the weather is not so warm.

For the topping
2 oz (50 g) butter, softened
2 oz (50 g) light muscovado sugar
15 oz (425 g) can of pear halves, drained
16 walnut halves

For the pudding
4 oz (100 g) soft margarine
4 oz (100 g) caster sugar
4 oz (100 g) self-raising flour
1½ level tablespoons cocoa, sieved
1 level teaspoon baking powder
2 eggs
a little milk

Heat the oven to 350°F/180°C/Gas Mark 4.

Prepare the topping: cream the butter and sugar together and spread over the base and sides of an 8–9-inch (20.5–23 cm) round cake tin. Arrange the pears and nuts cut-side down in the tin.

Place all the pudding ingredients together in a bowl and beat well for 2 minutes or until evenly blended. Spoon over the pears, smooth the top and bake in the oven for about 45 minutes, or until the pudding has shrunk slightly from the sides of the tin and the top springs back when pressed with a finger.

To freeze: *cool in the tin, cover with foil, label and freeze.*
To serve: *unwrap and leave to thaw at room temperature for 2–3 hours. Place in a moderate oven (350°F/180°C/Gas Mark 4) to warm through, about 20 minutes. Turn out and serve.*
Microwave: *defrost 3–4 minutes; reheat 3–4 minutes.*

Chocolate and Pear Upside-down Pudding; Oranges in Caramel Sauce

ORANGES IN CARAMEL SAUCE

Serves 6–8

Oranges and caramel sauce are a lovely combination and make a nice light finish to a heavy meal.

8 oz (225 g) granulated sugar
¼ pint (150 ml) cold water
¼ pint (150 ml) warm water
6–8 large seedless oranges

Place the sugar and cold water in a strong saucepan and cook over a low heat until the sugar has dissolved. Bring to the boil and cook steadily until a golden brown, then remove the pan from the heat. Hold the saucepan (covering your hand with an oven glove) over a bowl of lukewarm water and then add the warm water. Replace the saucepan over the heat and stir until the caramel has dissolved. Pour into a bowl to cool.

Using a potato peeler, pare a little rind from the skin of 1 orange and cut it into fine strips. Place in a saucepan, cover with cold water and cook for a minute. Drain and dry on kitchen paper.

Slice both ends from the oranges, then, standing the fruit upright on a plate, slice down and around the oranges to remove all the peel and pith. Slice across.

To freeze: *lay the oranges in a plastic box and pour over the caramel sauce. Cover, label and freeze. Freeze the strips of orange rind in a bag.*
To serve: *leave to thaw overnight in the refrigerator and then turn into a glass serving dish, sprinkle with the strips of orange rind and serve well chilled.*
Microwave: *defrost 3–4 minutes.*

RASPBERRY CHARLOTTE

(Pictured on the back cover)
Serves 8

This is a very good-looking pudding, and is ideal to serve at a dinner party.

15 oz (425 g) can of raspberries
½ oz (15 g) packet of powdered gelatine
juice of ½ lemon
1 packet (18) sponge finger or boudoir biscuits
2 eggs
2 oz (50 g) caster sugar
¼ pint (150 ml) double cream, whipped

🍴 *a little cream, whipped*
a few raspberries

Drain the raspberries and reserve the juice. Place 3 tablespoons of the juice in a small bowl with the gelatine and leave to stand for 3 minutes to form a sponge. Place the bowl over a pan of simmering water and stir to dissolve the gelatine. Add to the remaining fruit juice with the lemon juice and mix well. Pour a thin layer, about ¼ inch (5 mm), over the base of a 6-inch (15 cm) deep cake tin and leave to set in a cool place. Then arrange the biscuits around the side of the tin, with the sugar sides outside.

Sieve the raspberries and add the purée to the juice mixture, then stir until evenly blended and leave to stand until the mixture is about to set at the edges.

Meanwhile, put the eggs and sugar in a bowl and place over a pan of gently simmering water, whisking until the mixture is thick and leaves a trail when the whisk has been lifted out. Remove from the heat and leave to cool, whisking occasionally. Fold in the raspberry mixture and the cream until evenly blended and then turn into the prepared tin. Leave to set in the refrigerator.

To freeze: *cover with a lid of foil, label and freeze. Place the tin carefully in the freezer so that it will not get damaged. Use within 1 month.*
🍴 ***To serve:*** *leave to thaw in the refrigerator for 7 hours. Trim the tops of the biscuits so that they are level with the mousse. Loosen around the edge of the tin and dip into hot water for a few seconds to loosen the jelly. Turn out on to a serving dish and serve decorated with raspberries and a little whipped cream.*
Microwave: *defrost 3–5 minutes.*

APPLE PANCAKE ROLLS

Serves 8

I often make these with windfall apples from the garden.

For the filling
1 lb (450 g) cooking apples, peeled and sliced
4 oz (100 g) demerara sugar
2 oz (50 g) butter
½ level teaspoon mixed spice
4 oz (100 g) raisins
grated rind and juice of ½ small lemon

For the pancakes
4 oz (100 g) plain flour
1 egg
1 tablespoon sunflower oil, plus a little extra for frying
½ pint (300 ml) milk

🍴 *approx. 3 oz (75 g) butter*
cream or ice cream

Place the apples in a saucepan with the sugar, butter and spice and simmer gently, stirring occasionally, for about 20 minutes until tender. Stir in the raisins, lemon rind and juice and then turn into a bowl and leave to cool.

Now make the pancakes: place the flour in a bowl and make a well in the centre. Beat the egg with the oil and add to the bowl with half the milk; then, using a whisk, blend in the flour from the sides of the bowl. Beat well until the mixture is smooth, then stir in the remaining milk.

Heat a very little oil in an 8-inch (20 cm) frying pan. When it is hot, pour off any excess oil and spoon about 2 tablespoons of the batter into the pan. Tip and rotate so that the batter spreads out and thinly covers the base of the pan. Cook the pancake for 1 minute until pale brown, then turn over and cook the other side. Turn out and make 7 more pancakes.

Divide the filling between the pancakes and roll up.

Apple Pancake Rolls; Spicy Apricot Tart

To freeze: *wrap in a double thickness of foil, seal and label.*
🍴 ***To serve:*** *unwrap the pancakes; leave to thaw at room temperature for about 4 hours. Melt the butter in a frying pan and fry the pancake rolls on all sides until they are an even golden brown. Serve with lots of cream or ice cream.*
Microwave: *defrost 5 minutes and fry as directed.*

SPICY APRICOT TART

Serves 6

If you like, try making this tart using peaches, pears or apples.

For the pastry
4 oz (100 g) plain flour, plus extra for rolling
1 oz (25 g) margarine, cut in small pieces
1 oz (25 g) lard, cut in small pieces
approx. 4 teaspoons cold water

For the filling
15 oz (425 g) can of apricots
4 oz (100 g) plain flour
1 oz (25 g) ground almonds
2½ oz (65 g) butter
1½ oz (40 g) caster sugar
¼ teaspoon cinnamon

Heat the oven to 400°F/200°C/Gas Mark 6.

Place the flour for the pastry in a bowl, add the pieces of fat and rub in until the mixture resembles fine breadcrumbs. Add sufficient cold water to mix to a firm dough. Roll out the pastry on a floured table and use to line a 7-inch (18 cm) fluted flan tin.

Drain the apricots and arrange half over the base of the tart. Place the flour and almonds in a bowl and rub in the butter until the mixture resembles breadcrumbs, then stir in the sugar and cinnamon.

Cover the apricots with a layer of the almond mixture, place the rest of the apricots on top and cover with the remaining almond mixture, pressing down firmly.

Bake in the oven for 15 minutes, then reduce the oven

temperature to 325°F/170°C/Gas Mark 3 and cook for a further 30 minutes until the tart is golden brown and crisp.

To freeze: *cool quickly, wrap in foil, label and freeze.*
To serve: *thaw at room temperature for 5–6 hours and either serve cold or, how I like it, warmed through in a cool oven (300°F/150°C/Gas Mark 2) and served with a bowl of whipped cream.*
Microwave: *defrost 5–6 minutes; reheat 3 minutes.*

PEARS DELICE

(Pictured on the back cover)
Serves 6
This dish is delicious served with a bowl of lightly whipped cream.

6 oz (175 g) granulated sugar
¾ pint (450 ml) water
4 large pears
8 oz (225 g) fresh raspberries

Place the sugar and water in a shallow saucepan, heat gently until the sugar has dissolved and bring to the boil.

Peel, quarter and core the pears and place in the sugar syrup, then reduce the heat and poach the pears gently for about 15–20 minutes or until just tender. (The cooking time varies with the variety of pear used.) Carefully lift out the pears with a slotted spoon and place in a rigid container.

Sieve the raspberries into a bowl and stir in ¼ pint (150 ml) of the sugar syrup, stirring until evenly blended. Pour over the pears and leave to cool.

To freeze: *cover, label and freeze.*
To serve: *leave to thaw at room temperature for about 3 hours and then turn into a serving dish and keep in the refrigerator until required.*
Microwave: *defrost 3–5 minutes.*

DATE AND APPLE PIE

Serves 4–6

For a change, use raisins or prunes instead of dates.

1½ lb (675 g) cooking apples, peeled, cored and sliced
4 oz (100 g) light soft brown sugar
2 oz (50 g) butter
½ level teaspoon ground cinnamon
4 oz (100 g) stoned dates

For the pastry
8 oz (225 g) plain flour
2 oz (50 g) margarine, cut in small pieces
2 oz (50 g) lard, cut in small pieces
approx. 8 teaspoons cold water

🍴 *a little milk*

Put the apples in a saucepan with the sugar, butter and cinnamon. Cook gently until the apples are just tender, stirring occasionally. Remove from the heat, stir in the dates and leave to cool.

For the pastry: place the flour in a bowl, add the pieces of fat and rub in with the fingertips until the mixture resembles breadcrumbs. Add sufficient cold water to make a firm dough. Divide the pastry in two. Roll out one piece to line an 8-inch (20 cm) foil plate and spread in the apple mixture. Moisten the edges with water, roll out and cover with the remaining pastry and then press the edges together well to seal.

To freeze: *open-freeze, cover with a lid of foil, label and return to the freezer.*

🍴 ***To serve:*** *remove the wrapping, make two slits in the top of the pie, brush with a little milk and bake in the oven at 425°F/220°C/Gas Mark 7 for about 30–40 minutes.*

CHILLED ORANGE CHEESECAKE

(Pictured on the back cover)

Serves 8

This is a nice, easy cheesecake to make. Serve all the year round and decorate with fresh fruit as in season.

1 packet of orange jelly
6 oz (175 g) digestive biscuits
3 oz (75 g) butter
1 oz (25 g) demerara sugar
¼ pint (150 ml) double cream
12 oz (350 g) cream cheese
juice of 1 orange
4 oz (100 g) caster sugar

Break the jelly into cubes and place in a measuring jug. Make up to ¼ pint (150 ml) with boiling water and stir until dissolved. Make up to ½ pint (300 ml) with cold water and leave in a cool place until starting to set.

Put the biscuits in a bag and crush with a rolling pin. Melt the butter in a saucepan and stir in the biscuit crumbs and demerara sugar. Press over the base of an 8-inch (20 cm) loose-bottomed, round cake tin.

Whisk the cream until it is thick and forms soft peaks. Place the cream cheese in a bowl and beat with a wooden spoon until soft and creamy, then beat in the orange juice, caster sugar and the setting jelly and finally fold in the cream. Turn the mixture into the tin and place in the refrigerator until set.

To freeze: *cover with a double thickness of foil, label and freeze.*
To serve: *leave to thaw overnight in the refrigerator and then place on a serving dish and serve decorated with fruit and cream.*
Microwave: *defrost 3–5 minutes, checking after each minute.*

Cakes and Bakes

'Bake now and eat later' is a perfect rule for cakes and bakes, as almost all baked food will freeze well. Have a morning cooking and freeze on the same day for the best results. I like to stock up my cake and biscuit tins and then pack the remainder away in the freezer.

Wrap up cakes carefully and pack in rigid containers – sometimes I cut a cake into portions before freezing, separating the slices with freezer film or waxed paper. This is a handy way to have a cake stored, as you can just remove the portions you need and the thawing time is speeded up considerably.

Guests often seem to pop in unexpectedly during the weekends and I find it very useful to have scones in the freezer, as they thaw quickly or can even be popped straight into the oven before being served with a dish of home-made jam.

CHOCOLATE FORK BISCUITS

Makes approx. 36

Use butter to make these biscuits because the flavour really does come through.

8 oz (225 g) butter
4 oz (100 g) light soft brown sugar
1 teaspoon vanilla essence
8 oz (225 g) self-raising flour
2 oz (50 g) drinking chocolate

Cream the butter with the sugar and vanilla essence until really soft and creamy, then work in the flour and drinking chocolate. Divide the mixture into pieces the size of a walnut and roll into balls. Place them on a baking sheet and flatten with a fork which has been dipped into cold water.

To freeze: *open-freeze, pack into a rigid container, cover, label and return to the freezer.*
To serve: *cook straight from the freezer, placed on greased baking trays and baked in the oven at 375°F/190°C/Gas Mark 5 for about 12–15 minutes. Leave to cool on the trays for a minute or two and then lift on to a wire rack to finish cooling.*

CHOCOLATE FUDGE LAYER CAKE

This is a lovely chocolate cake that freezes well.

For the cake
a little oil for greasing
2 level tablespoons cocoa
2 tablespoons hot water
4 oz (100 g) soft margarine
4 oz (100 g) light muscovado sugar
2 large eggs
4 oz (100 g) self-raising flour
1 level teaspoon baking powder

For the icing
3 oz (75 g) butter
2 oz (50 g) cocoa, sieved
5 tablespoons milk
8 oz (225 g) icing sugar, sieved

Heat the oven to 350°F/180°C/Gas Mark 4. Grease and line with greased greaseproof paper two 7-inch (18 cm) sandwich tins.

Blend the cocoa with the hot water in a large bowl and leave to cool. Add the remaining cake ingredients and beat well with a wooden spoon for about 2 minutes until blended.

Divide the mixture between the tins and bake in the oven for 25–30 minutes. When cooked, the cake will have shrunk slightly from the sides of the tin and will spring back when pressed with a finger. Turn out, remove the paper and leave to cool on a wire rack. Split each cake in half horizontally.

Now make the icing: melt the butter in a small

saucepan, stir in the cocoa and cook for a minute. Remove the pan from the heat, stir in the milk and icing sugar and beat well to mix. Leave to cool, stirring occasionally, until thick and of a spreading consistency.

Sandwich together each layer of cake with a quarter of the icing. Spread the top piece of cake with the remaining icing and swirl attractively.

To freeze: *open-freeze, then place in a polythene bag, seal, label and return to the freezer.*
To serve: *unwrap, place on a plate and leave to thaw at room temperature for 3–4 hours.*
Microwave: *defrost 3–4 minutes, checking after each minute.*

MOCHA BARS

Makes 20

Coffee and chocolate is a good combination and these cakes make an ideal contribution to a coffee morning.

a little oil for greasing
6 oz (175 g) soft margarine
6 oz (175 g) caster sugar
3 eggs
3 oz (75 g) plain chocolate, grated coarsely
1 tablespoon coffee essence
6 oz (175 g) self-raising flour
1½ level teaspoons baking powder

For the icing
3 oz (75 g) soft margarine
8 oz (225 g) icing sugar, sieved
1 tablespoon hot water
1 tablespoon coffee essence
1 oz (25 g) chocolate, grated

Heat the oven to 325°F/170°C/Gas Mark 3. Grease and line a large tin, 12 × 9 inches (30.5 × 23 cm), with greased greaseproof paper.

Chocolate Fudge Layer Cake; Mocha Bars; Chocolate Fork Biscuits

Place all the cake ingredients in a large bowl and beat well until smooth and blended. Turn out the prepared tin and smooth the top. Bake in the oven for about 40 minutes or until the cake is well risen and shrinking away from the sides of the tin. Leave to cool in the tin.

For the icing: put the margarine, icing sugar, water and coffee essence in a bowl and beat until smooth. Spread over the cake and sprinkle with the grated chocolate, pressing it in lightly so that it doesn't come off. Cut into 20 bars.

To freeze: *pack carefully into firm containers in a single layer, cover, label and freeze.*
To serve: *leave to thaw at room temperature for 1–2 hours.*
Microwave: *defrost in batches for 2--3 minutes.*

SHORTBREAD FINGERS

(Pictured on page 15)
Makes 16
I like to keep a batch of these in the freezer as they are so good to serve with mousses, fools and whips.

a little oil for greasing
4 oz (100 g) plain flour
2 oz (50 g) ground rice
4 oz (100 g) butter
2 oz (50 g) caster sugar

caster or icing sugar, for dusting

Heat the oven to 325°F/170°C/Gas Mark 3. Grease a shallow tin, 11 × 7 inches (28 × 18 cm).

Sieve the flour and ground rice together in a bowl, rub in the butter with the fingertips until the mixture resembles breadcrumbs and stir in the sugar. Work the mixture until it all comes together, turn on to a work surface and knead well until smooth and silky.

Press into the tin evenly, using the back of a damp spoon or your knuckles.

Bake in the oven for about 15–20 minutes until the

shortbread is a very pale golden brown. Remove from the oven and cut into 16 fingers. Leave to cool in the tin.

To freeze: *place in a container, cover, label and freeze.*
To serve: *leave to thaw at room temperature for 3–4 hours and dust with caster or icing sugar before serving.*
Microwave: *defrost 2–3 minutes.*

SCONES

Makes approx. 10–12

When making scones be sure that the mixture is not too dry and try not to handle the dough too much. I always keep a batch in the freezer ready for a Sunday tea in front of the fire, and top them with some of this year's home-made jam.

a little oil for greasing
8 oz (225 g) self-raising flour, plus extra for flouring
1 level teaspoon baking powder
2 oz (50 g) soft margarine
1 oz (25 g) caster sugar
1 egg
approx. ¼ pint (150 ml) milk

Heat the oven to 425°F/220°C/Gas Mark 7. Lightly grease a baking sheet.

Put the flour and baking powder in a bowl, add the margarine and rub in with the fingertips until the mixture resembles fine breadcrumbs. Stir in the sugar.

Break the egg into a measure, lightly beat it and then make up to ¼ pint (150 ml) with milk. Stir the egg and milk into the flour and mix to a soft dough. Turn on to a lightly floured surface, knead lightly and roll out to ½ inch (1 cm) thickness.

Cut the scones into rounds with a 2½-inch (6 cm) fluted cutter to make about 10–12 scones. Place on the baking sheet, brush the tops with a little milk and bake for about 10 minutes or until a pale golden brown. Leave to cool on a wire rack.

To freeze: *pack into a polythene bag, seal, label and freeze.*

To serve: *if in a hurry, take straight from the deep freeze, place on a baking sheet and reheat in a hot oven (425°F/220°C/Gas Mark 7) for about 10 minutes. If time allows, leave to thaw at room temperature for about 2 hours and then warm through in a cool oven (300°F/150°C/Gas Mark 2).*
Microwave: *defrost four at a time for 1–2 minutes.*

FRUIT CAKE

A fruit cake keeps well in the deep freeze and I often prepare one to keep ready for holidays.

a little oil for greasing
6 oz (175 g) soft margarine
5 oz (150 g) light muscovado sugar
3 eggs
7 oz (200 g) self-raising flour
1 level teaspoon baking powder
2 tablespoons sherry
1 oz (25 g) ground almonds
1 lb (450 g) mixed dried fruit

Heat the oven to 325°F/170°C/Gas Mark 3. Line with greased greaseproof paper a 7-inch (18 cm) round cake tin.

Cream the margarine and sugar together until soft and creamy and then beat in the eggs one at a time. Fold in the flour and baking powder and then the sherry and ground almonds. Fold in the dried fruit. Turn the mixture into the tin and smooth the top.

Bake in the oven for about 2½ hours until the cake is a deep golden brown and a skewer pierced in the centre comes out clean. Leave to cool in the tin for about 30 minutes before turning out and removing the paper. Leave on a wire rack to finish cooling.

To freeze: *wrap in a double thickness of foil, label and freeze.*
To serve: *leave to thaw at room temperature, unwrapped, for about 8 hours.*
Microwave: *defrost 4–5 minutes.*

Fruit Cake; Scones

GRANARY ROLLS

Makes 16 big rolls or 20–24 smaller rolls

I make the dough and then shape it into 16 big rolls, which seem to be the best size for my hungry family. If you are not feeding teenagers, I suggest that you divide the dough into 20–24 pieces and make the rolls slightly smaller.

1 teaspoon sugar
just under ¾ pint (450 ml) hand-hot water
3 level teaspoons dried yeast
12 oz (350 g) strong plain flour, plus extra for flouring
12 oz (350 g) granary flour, plus extra for dusting
3 level teaspoons salt
1 tablespoon sunflower oil, plus a little extra for greasing

Dissolve the sugar in the water and then sprinkle on the yeast and leave to stand for 10 minutes until frothy.

Put the flours and salt in a large bowl, pour on the yeast and oil and mix well to form a dough that will leave the sides of the bowl clean.

Turn on to a floured table and knead until smooth and no longer sticky – this will take about 10 minutes. Fold the dough towards you, then push down with the palm of the hand. Give the dough a quarter turn and repeat the kneading, developing a rocking rhythm and continuing until the dough feels firm and elastic. Shape into a large ball, place in a large polythene bag greased with a little oil and leave in a warm place to rise until doubled in bulk. This will take about 1 hour in a warm place.

Turn the dough on to a lightly floured table, divide in half and flatten with the knuckles to knock out the air. Divide each piece of dough into the required number of pieces and shape into rolls. Place evenly spaced on a greased baking sheet, put in a greased polythene bag and leave to double in bulk.

Dust the rolls with a little granary flour and bake in the oven at 425°F/220°C/Gas Mark 7 for about 15–20 minutes. If you have made smaller rolls, cut down the cooking time by about 3–4 minutes. The cooked rolls will be golden brown and will sound hollow if tapped on the base.

Place on a wire rack on top of a clean tea-towel, cover with another tea-towel and leave to cool. This keeps the rolls soft.

To freeze: *pack in a polythene bag, seal and label.*
To serve: *place straight in the oven on a baking sheet and cook at 300°F/150°C/Gas Mark 2 for about 15 minutes or until fully thawed. Or, leave to thaw at room temperature for about 2 hours and then put in a 300°F/150°C/Gas Mark 2 oven for about 10 minutes to warm the rolls through.*
Microwave: *defrost four at a time for 2 minutes.*

GARLIC BREAD

Serves 6–8

This is great to have in the freezer, but do not keep longer than a week to ten days as garlic tends to go musty in the freezer.

2 cloves of garlic, crushed
a little salt and freshly ground black pepper
4 oz (100 g) butter
1 teaspoon chopped parsley
1 teaspoon chopped mixed herbs
1 french loaf

Put the garlic, salt, pepper and butter in a bowl, cream together until soft and fully blended and then beat in the herbs. Cut the french bread almost through to the base in 1-inch (2.5 cm) slices. Spread between the slices with the garlic butter and then press the loaf back into shape.

To freeze: *wrap in a double thickness of foil, label and freeze.*
To serve: *thaw at room temperature for 3–4 hours and then heat, still in the foil, in a 400°F/200°C/Gas Mark 6 oven for about 15 minutes, when the bread will be hot through and crisp and the garlic butter melted.*
Microwave: *defrost 2–3 minutes.*

CHEESE STRAWS

These are very handy to have in the deep freeze, as they can be served with drinks and make a good accompaniment for soup.

8 oz (225 g) plain flour, plus extra for flouring
salt and pepper
a little cayenne pepper (optional)
4 oz (100 g) butter
4 oz (100 g) well flavoured Cheddar cheese, grated finely
a little beaten egg

Heat the oven to 400°F/200°C/Gas Mark 6. Lightly grease 2 or 3 large baking sheets.

Put the flour in a bowl with the salt and pepper (if you like, also add a little cayenne pepper). Add the butter, cut in small pieces, and rub in with the fingertips until the mixture resembles fine breadcrumbs. Stir in the cheese. Add sufficient beaten egg to make a firm dough, turn out on to a floured surface and knead lightly until the mixture is smooth.

Roll out to approximately ¼ inch (5 mm) thickness and cut the pastry into narrow strips, rings, circles or fancy shapes such as diamonds. Carefully lift on to the baking sheets and cook in the oven for 8–10 minutes or until a pale golden brown. Leave on the baking sheets for a minute or two and then lift on to a wire rack to finish cooling.

To freeze: *pack in a rigid container, seal, label and freeze.*
To serve: *allow to thaw at room temperature for about 1 hour or, for speed, warm through in a moderate oven (350°F/180°C/Gas Mark 4) for about 5 minutes.*
Microwave: *defrost 1–2 minutes.*

Granary Rolls; Garlic Bread; Cheese Straws

Index to recipes